Refilled

FINDING *fullness* IN GOD
WHEN LIFE LEAVES YOU *empty*

KRISTINE BROWN

Refilled

FINDING *fullness* IN GOD WHEN LIFE LEAVES YOU *empty*

Aberdeen Books LLC

Copyright 2025 by Kristine Brown

Published by Aberdeen Books, LLC, Tyler, Texas

All rights reserved. No part of this publication may be reproduced, distributed, or transmitted in any form or by any means, including photocopying, recording, or other electronic or mechanical methods, without the prior written permission of the publisher, except in the case of brief quotations embodied in critical reviews and certain other noncommercial uses permitted by copyright law. Requests for permission can be addressed to: Permissions, Aberdeen Books, 1910 E SE Loop 323 #231, Tyler, TX, 75701

ISBN: 978-1-7375986-3-3

Library of Congress Control Number: 2024921368

Unless otherwise indicated, Scripture quotations are from The ESV® Bible (The Holy Bible, English Standard Version®), copyright © 2001 by Crossway, a publishing ministry of Good News Publishers. Used by permission. All rights reserved.

Scripture quotations marked NLT are taken from the Holy Bible, New Living Translation, copyright ©1996, 2004, 2015 by Tyndale House Foundation. Used by permission of Tyndale House Publishers, Carol Stream, Illinois 60188. All rights reserved.

Scripture quotations marked NIV are taken from THE HOLY BIBLE, NEW INTERNATIONAL VERSION®, NIV® Copyright © 1973, 1978, 1984, 2011 by Biblica, Inc.® Used by permission. All rights reserved worldwide.

Scripture quotations taken from the Amplified® Bible (AMP), Copyright © 2015 by The Lockman Foundation. Used by permission. www.lockman.org.

Scripture quotations marked HCSB are taken from the Holman Christian Standard Bible®, Used by Permission HCSB ©1999, 2000, 2002, 2003, 2009 Holman Bible Publishers. Holman Christian Standard Bible®, Holman CSB®, and HCSB® are federally registered trademarks of Holman Bible Publishers.

Scripture quotations from the COMMON ENGLISH BIBLE. © Copyright 2011 COMMON ENGLISH BIBLE. All rights reserved. Used by permission. (www.CommonEnglishBible.com).

Scripture quotations marked TPT are from The Passion Translation®. Copyright © 2017, 2018, 2020 by Passion & Fire Ministries, Inc. Used by permission. All rights reserved. ThePassionTranslation.com.

Scripture quotations marked CEV are from the Contemporary English Version, Copyright © 1991, 1992, 1995 by American Bible Society. Used by Permission.

Cover & Interior Design by Five Js Design, fivejsdesign.com

TABLE OF CONTENTS

Introduction | 9

CHAPTER 1	Empty Spaces	15
CHAPTER 2	The Lonely Heart Club	33
CHAPTER 3	A Little Less Full	47
CHAPTER 4	An Omer of Good Things	61
CHAPTER 5	Give Me Strength!	75
CHAPTER 6	Bitter Woman	91
CHAPTER 7	So, Help Me, God	105
CHAPTER 8	Even More	121
CHAPTER 9	In a New Light	135
CHAPTER 10	Down in My Heart, Where?	147
CHAPTER 11	Jesus Fills Me, This I Know	161
CHAPTER 12	A Life Refilled	173

Appendix A: Reflection Pages | 183

Appendix B: Book Club Reading Plan | 197

Notes | 199

Acknowledgments | 203

Connect with Kristine | 205

Introduction

"Lord, I've been sensing a void lately that I can't quite explain…"

I clipped the words from a devotion I'd written for an online magazine and posted them on social media. The short prayer expressed the cry of my weary spirit. It felt as if someone had taken a shovel to my heart and carved out a space, then left behind a vacancy that had never been filled. It had been there so long, it became part of me. Until now, I'd learned to coexist with it, but praying about the void made me realize how hard it was to describe or even understand why it was there. I prayed because I had more questions than answers and hoped for an easy fix, a quick resolution from God to soothe the aching. Maybe he'd even provide a way to bring back the missing piece and mirror the life I once knew.

I wasn't sure what prompted me to tell others about my void. Maybe I wanted to know I wasn't the only one with a nagging emptiness that wouldn't go away, or maybe I longed to have someone pray for me. Strength in numbers, and all that. But I didn't expect to see comments and messages pouring in from friends who could relate to the void I mentioned in my prayer—friends who loved the Lord and thanked him daily for his blessings, but still didn't feel whole. I realized then and there, it was time to dig in to God's Word and see what he had to say about this mutual longing in our hearts. That's where the idea for the *Refilled* book began.

Those of you who've been with me for a while know how much I love connecting women today with women of the Bible, sharing their stories in a way that bonds us together. It's one of my most persistent callings and also my greatest joys. Even though a vast stretch divides our modern culture from their traditions, we find common ground in our feelings, experiences, and opportunities to grow closer to our Lord.

If this is your first time picking up a book I've written, thank you for trusting me to guide you deeper into what God wants us to discover about his promises for our empty spaces. I believe he has remarkable insight waiting. And as we turn each page, we are trusting him to be our Ultimate Guide. The places he has prepared for us may sometimes be rocky, but they are perfectly designed for our individual needs. God has good things in store. That is his promise to us.

Before we begin, allow me to open up to you about a few things. Please know this nonfiction book has been prayed over, agonized over, and crafted for the sole purpose of helping us rely on God more and draw closer to him in our everyday lives. Because I included so much Scripture and historical background, you may decide to use this book as a Bible study on the Book of Ruth instead, and that's okay. Grab a journal and your favorite pen, record each verse shared, and learn new things! I believe it pleases God when we open the Bible with a hunger and thirst for knowledge.

In addition to drawing closer to God, chances are we will also feel a connectedness with one another. Even though right now you are on the other side of the page, I have prayed for you, the *Refilled* reader, and the journey on which we're about to embark. After reading, if you'd like to stay connected, I've included ways to do just that in the back of the book. Learning and growing is more fun with friends.

You'll notice as you read, sometimes I like to illustrate a scene from a biblical woman's life in narrative form, telling her story by bringing her experiences to life in a fresh way. You can rest assured, extensive research and study goes into the background of each book I write. I explore what life was like for women back then, including things like the clothes they wore, their daily chores, their roles in the home and society, and what was happening around them at the time. I use that research to write in such a way that we feel as though we are walking alongside them, doing what they do and seeing what they see. Immersing ourselves in their struggles and victories strengthens our connection and helps us relate to their stories. I pray you enjoy your time here, and that God will give you many "a-ha" moments along the way.

Why Naomi?

As I began my own personal journey through the Book of Ruth, I came across this sentence in my *Life Application Study Bible*, "Not much is said about Naomi except that she loved and cared for Ruth."

I had to read the words again to make sure I'd read them right. My argumentative side surfaced. I shook my head and thought, "What do you mean *not much is written*? There's a wealth of information about Naomi in here!" You'll be glad to know I got hold of myself and stopped short of writing a letter to the editor.

Then I noticed that somehow, those words express how we all feel sometimes, as if someone looked back at our life story and quipped, "Not much is said about her. Nothing worth mentioning, anyway." We spend our days loving and caring for others—cooking meals, sorting laundry, checking homework, consoling and comforting, scheduling activities, and punching a time clock. Yet, we can live as if we never did anything noteworthy. Missed opportunities, mistakes of the past, or losses we had no control over lie to us by whispering our time here hasn't added up to much.

But just like God had a wealth of inspiration and wisdom to impart through the life of Naomi in the Bible, he also has an abundance of good things to say about you and me. Our lives are a story still being written, and I can confidently say, we will see many of those good things unearthed in the pages ahead.

Because here's the thing. Something drew Ruth to Naomi. Something powerful and fascinating and uniquely beautiful. As I continued reading through the "Introduction to Ruth" in

INTRODUCTION

my study Bible, I sighed with relief as the quote went on to say, "Naomi's life was a powerful witness to the reality of God."

So here's the gist: there would be no story of Ruth without Naomi.

There. I said it. And while I'm feeling bold, I'll add this. We are on the verge of receiving a heaping mound of encouragement from Naomi's powerful witness, and I cannot wait.

Countless books and studies have been written on Ruth, and rightfully so. The book we're about to walk through in the Bible bears her name, after all. But my quest to find books all about Naomi left me empty-handed. You now hold in your hands the culmination of my journey with this no-nonsense woman of faith and what she taught me about living a life refilled. I am beyond grateful to have you here.

Thank you for joining me, from the bottom of my heart. There's no place I'd rather be right now, and no one I'd rather be with on this adventure—you, me, Naomi, and God. So grab your gear, fellow sojourner. It's time to take our first steps.

REFILLED

CHAPTER 1

Empty Spaces

"The Lord is my chosen portion and my cup; you hold my lot"

PSALM 16:5

I watched the scene unfold in earth tones dotted with vibrant orange. Time and space faded. I viewed the film from the comfort of my chair, but felt as if I was there, transported to the fictional world created by author Louis Sachar and adapted for the big screen. The antagonist stepped into play with her dust-covered boots and a glare that could scare a snake. Even though I knew the story by heart, I held my breath...

Sarcasm dripped with each word the "Warden" spoke. Her feminine drawl emphasized her authority over all the happenings at Camp Green Lake.[1]

She had told...scratch that. She had *ordered* Mr. Pendanski, the camp counselor, to fill the campers' water jugs. When he responded, "I've already filled them," she ambled toward her lowly employee, an intimidation tactic, for sure. Then, the Warden grabbed one camper's jug and shook it with conviction.

She mocked, "Can ya hear the empty spaces?"

Even with a few sips missing from the dirty makeshift water bottle, the rest of the contents sloshed about, making the empty spaces evident to anyone within earshot. The result—a ruckus caused by emptiness.[2]

Sometimes my heart can feel a lot like that water jug in the hands of a merciless warden.

I wake up with a pang in my chest that won't subside, a physical reminder of a priceless treasure I once had that's now gone. The nagging void will not stop hurting, no matter how much I try to focus on everything else around it.

Some days, the water settles. Stillness finds its home, and I can be fooled by the illusion my heart is full. I'll post a quick picture for everyone to see all is right in my world, for the moment. But that picture never tells the whole story. The smile on my face is real, and the feeling of fullness in my heart seems just as real, but at the day's end when all the fun has been captured and the phone battery dies, the empty spaces return.

Not that I'm complaining. When good feelings emerge and things are going well with my people, I'll be the first to say I'm abundantly blessed. I like to remind myself of that, because most days I live with the pang I mentioned before. The heart-full days are sprinkled throughout the monotony of long, parched seasons. It's as if most of life shakes and churns, causing a constant, painful reminder of one thing: the void in my heart that needs to be filled.

CHAPTER 1 — EMPTY SPACES

No matter how much I pray, distract myself, or wish it away, that painful void never leaves. I wonder if relief is out there somewhere or if I should just learn to live with it.

WHY WE ALL HAVE EMPTY SPACES

In the scene I described above from the movie adaptation of the book *Holes*, Mr. Pendanski could easily remedy the problem of empty spaces by holding the old, recycled milk jug under the water spout for a few seconds. Problem solved. If only filling the void in our hearts were that easy.

Let me take a quick detour right here to issue a disclaimer for us all. I believe thankfulness is a vital component to finding contentment in this life. It's also a daily habit, and I don't know where I'd be without it. Each new season of life gives us plenty of reasons to be thankful. If I asked you to name three things you're thankful for right now, you could probably come up with way more than three. Maybe like me, you'd say things like: my marriage, my kids, friends and family, or even a beautiful sunrise on a warm day. Then you might dig a little deeper and remember how God brought you through a health battle. How he reconnected you with loved ones you thought would never speak to you again. Or maybe how he gave you that opportunity to go to college, helped you get a job you wanted, or allowed you to serve in a ministry.

So many blessings, they're almost immeasurable. But each new season also exposes our hearts to the possibility of losing something we once had. Each loss creates another empty space representing deep hurt in need of even deeper healing.

That is the topic of this book, my faith friend. Loss leaves behind a void like an elusive missing last jigsaw puzzle piece after you've spent hours in tedious assembly. No matter how you look at the beautiful image formed by all the pieces joined together so neatly, the picture will never be complete.

There are endless circumstances in our lives that can leave behind these empty spaces. Long distances pull us away from the people, places, and familiarity we once knew. Our kids grow and leave as we struggle to navigate the empty nest. Death causes a chasm of grief and pain. The remnants of health issues mean we can't do our favorite things anymore. Retirement, divorce, or closing the lid on a dream unrealized because "life happens" all create empty spaces. I could name a few more, and I believe you could, too. But I'll stop here before going too deep. I wouldn't want to give you the idea that the pages ahead are all about what's missing. Instead, I want to move past my apprehension and ask you to do something difficult, but necessary.

I know how shocking it is to see that word—*difficult*—when easy sounds much more inviting, but we're beginning an important journey together, you and me. A journey toward discovering what to do with our emptiness. We will also be joined by a no-nonsense woman from the Bible (whom you will love, by the way) along with a few others, too.

So as we begin, I want us to have a solid understanding of our roles here. Don't think of me as a merciless warden, like at Camp Green Lake, untrustworthy in her selfish pursuit of treasure. I'm not Mr. Pendanski either, the unqualified camp counselor giving you advice you didn't ask for in the first place. If you haven't had the opportunity to read the book *Holes* or view the movie, I'll let you in on a little secret without spoiling the story for you. The Warden forces the campers to dig holes every day in the heat, without a reprieve.

So for our purposes here, let's think of ourselves as fellow campers in the struggle together. We're ready to lend a hand when the scorching sun gets to be too much, and the blisters on our hands won't heal. We may even need to carry one another through the rocky terrain from time to time, and that's okay because that's what campers do. We link arms, sing catchy songs, and encourage each other to keep going, even when we're so weary we can't lift the shovel. True replenishment awaits at the intersection of our parched places.

So I invite you to join me, fellow camper. Our journey starts now.

WHAT IT MEANS TO BE FILLED

"Fill my cup, Lord." I've heard those four words prayed many times from pulpits in churches, and I'm willing to assume you have, too. I've even sung the words in songs and seen them written on square images with pretty floral backgrounds. I've prayed this prayer in desperation and longing for relief. Yet, each time after I pray, I open my eyes and go about my day utterly unchanged. I know God has the power to fill my empty spaces and make them whole again, but I get complacent when it comes to recognizing his restoring work in my day-to-day life.

"The Lord is my chosen portion and my cup; you hold my lot" (Psalm 16:5).

The thought of a plain old cup brings all sorts of images to mind. I envision a thirsty toddler, downing the last drops from his sippy cup and still wanting more. Or a desperate soul sitting on the curbside, holding out a tin cup with a few measly clinks rattling around in the bottom. However you see the cup in front of you today, let's prepare ourselves to reframe that picture in our minds.

The above power-packed verse from the psalms will serve as our starting place. I believe it will stir our hearts and point us to soul-satisfying truths in God's Word. The Holman Christian Standard Bible (HCSB) describes our cup as "my cup of blessing." That's our personal cup, yours and mine. Changing our thinking from a simple cup to "my cup of blessing" expands our idea of what our cup, in God's capable hands, is all about.

God's presence, his very self, is our greatest blessing.

So why do we have a tough time believing that truth? If God is my forever cup of blessing, pouring his goodness fully into my life, why do I still ache from the void that won't go away? We will uncover the answer in this book, but first, let's prepare our hearts by digging into what it means to be filled, according to God's unchanging Word.

The *New Living Translation Bible Concordance* defines the word *fill* as, "to occupy the whole of, to spread through, or to supply fully." As we delve into seeking God's fullness, we are in the perfect place to expand our understanding of our Heavenly Father's plan for filling.[3] Let's look at these three definitions one at a time, so they can spark hope and anticipation for the road in front of us.

CHAPTER 1 — EMPTY SPACES

TO OCCUPY THE WHOLE OF

The land of promise stretched out before them like an endless sea of sustaining grace, a thing of beauty, waiting for its rightful owner to settle and care for it. There at the border, God's people stood, gazing ahead.

"Just look at this fruit!" the twelve men proclaimed as they returned and held out figs and pomegranates to show the crowd. They'd seen the beauty for themselves and brought back what they could carry. Forty days they had scoped out the situation for the sole purpose of reporting back to Moses. Now, the Israelites awaited the word. Would they forge ahead and occupy this land that really did flow with milk and honey?[4]

You may recall the next scene in this story. We talked about it in my book *Cinched*, when Joshua returned to lead God's people, a whopping forty years after they stood at the cusp of their destiny once before. We discovered how Moses had sent twelve men to spy out the land. Joshua was one of those men, and only one other voice voted to go forward, Caleb.

"But Caleb quieted the people before Moses and said, 'Let us go up at once and *occupy it*, for we are well able to overcome it'" (Numbers 13:30, Emphasis mine).

The people decided against following Joshua and Caleb's advice. Fear got the best of them, so this magnificent promise from God, full of sustenance and provision, would have to wait forty years. Unfortunately, that also meant this particular crowd of folks wouldn't get to experience it.

God intended his children's inheritance to be vast, beautiful, and full of promise. That includes his plan for you and me. Part

In the same way he called upon his people to occupy the land, God wants to occupy our whole heart.

of our inheritance in him is an abundant life where he provides for every need. That doesn't mean the fruit will always be plentiful or the bank account will always be stacked. But it does mean our inheritance rests in his mighty cupped hands. There's no better place it could be.

David expressed this thought with certainty and truth when he sang, "The Lord is my chosen portion and my cup; you hold my lot" (Psalm 16:5).

The Hebrew word for *lot* as it is used in this psalm is *goral*, meaning a "device by which a decision was made, an allotment (of land), portions, or allotted inheritance."[5] The *English Standard Version (ESV) Global Study Bible* puts it this way, "The psalmist is satisfied with the Lord and his provision. The terms portion, lot, lines, and inheritance recall the allocation of the Promised Land into tribal and family plots."

When fear gets the best of us, let's remember the psalmist's cry. He goes on to say, "I know the Lord is always with me. I will not be shaken, for he is right beside me" (Psalm 16:8 NLT).

In the same way he called upon his people to occupy the land, God wants to occupy our whole heart.

TO SPREAD THROUGH

I remember a day my young adult son called with unsettling news. After an episode of lightheadedness followed by a fall, doctors ordered a scan and discovered a cyst on his brain. It needed to be removed, sooner rather than later, but the medical climate at the time meant most surgeries were postponed indefinitely.

Surprisingly, that word "postponed" calmed my heart a little. I assumed if this was considered elective surgery, then the cyst couldn't be as dangerous as what my imagination would make it. I've been guilty in the past of chasing the worst-case scenario. Because of my tendency toward thinking the most horrible thing could happen, I got my focus in check by reminding myself God was bigger than this problem. I tried to picture a miniscule dot somewhere on the black-and-white image created by the MRI machine...nothing major to cause this momma too much concern.

During his appointment in the neurosurgeon's office, I laid eyes on the actual image. The familiar pang in my chest returned with a vengeance. A cyst wedged itself between his skull and brain like a water balloon ready to burst. It had likely been growing there most of his life, the doctor said. Yet, somehow we'd missed it until now.

"I cry to you, O Lord; I say, 'You are my refuge, my portion in the land of the living'" (Psalm 142:5).

For years I explored what it meant to live with God as my portion. I'd seen him described that way in Scripture and had prayed about what that phrase meant for me and the difficulties I faced. *My portion.* I wanted the words to be like a soothing balm over my pain, but instead I envisioned a pie with one slice missing—an illustration showing how each of us only receives a piece of the whole thing, regardless of our desire for more.

My own battle with cancer taught me a lot about the meaning of those words. Through lots of pain-filled downtime spent with Jesus and soaking in Scripture, I discovered measures God will pour into us when we don't know what to pray. But there was even more I needed to unearth. Now, as I sat beside my grown child and agonized over what he faced, I needed more than one measly slice of pie to get through this. Making medical decisions for myself in a life or death battle was hard enough, but supporting my child through *his* battle brought *hard* to a whole new level.

The day of his surgery, I stood alone just outside the front doors of the hospital. Restrictions kept visitors from gathering in the waiting areas. I marched around a circular fountain in the courtyard, my earbuds blasting the playlist of worship songs I'd downloaded in advance. Peace, strength, and comfort overcame me as I waited for news. Time passed faster than I expected (no doubt God had a hand in that), and I got the surgeon's call. The procedure had been successful. They released him to go home the next morning.

Six weeks later, we returned to that same office for a follow-up scan to see the results of the surgery. We witnessed something remarkable as we studied the new black-and-white image, enhanced by the back light shining through. My son's brain expanded into the area where the cyst had been. It filled the empty space, and the doctor predicted he would feel better, think better, and have a full recovery.

God knows what our heart needs, even when we don't. We can trust him to be our portion. We may ask him to fill us, but have no idea how he will answer. We will talk more about the beauty and specifics of living with God as our portion throughout this book, but for now we can rest in this truth. Whatever measure God uses to fill us, it will spread through the painful places and soothe our deepest hurts.

TO SUPPLY FULLY

What stands out in my memory most about that time in my son's life isn't the gut-wrenching decision over choosing the right surgeon. It isn't the questions over what side-effects might happen or even the startling horseshoe-shaped scar on the top of my son's head. Looking back, what comes to mind first is the water feature in the hospital's courtyard, a circular flowing fountain with concrete benches surrounding it. From any vantage point, you could look up and see desperate faces inside the hospital through the second story windows. Below them, the water calmed my heart in a continuous flow, filling the fountain in a never-ending supply stream.

If only the people beyond those hospital windows would glance down and see the hope of the fountain.

I'm thankful God helped me hold on to this piece of my son's story. The memory where I felt his Holy Spirit the most. Don't get me wrong, though. The word *craniotomy* can take a chunk out of even the most steadfast heart. I'd be kidding myself if I didn't admit feeling unnerved by that whole experience. But I've learned something deeply eye-opening from that day's events. The reason I felt God's presence so fully during the surgery is because I spent time in the preparation.

In the past I've tried time and again to prepare my heart for difficulties, both known and unknown. But when hard things happen (especially one after another), I fall back to old ways—

getting frustrated, losing sleep, and reacting in ways I later regret. Thankfully, our gracious God doesn't give up on us, no matter how many times we falter.

I believe this book is our preparation for difficulties, fellow camper.

We have a life-changing story ahead, filled with lessons designed to help us come to God with the hole in our heart. And just maybe, we will also begin to view the emptiness we feel with new readiness to receive from his endless supply.

Philippians 4:19 says, "And my God will supply every need of yours according to his riches in glory in Christ Jesus."

Just like the ever-flowing water, God promises to meet our needs. In my hours walking around the fountain, I needed peace, strength, and a whole list of other things. It was one of those rare times when I knew what would fill the void. However, there are also those times in our lives when we can't possibly know. Our heart cries out for help, but we don't have a clue what will satisfy. So let's envision the water flowing freely right now. Allow me to reach for your hand and lead you around the fountain, however many times it takes. Let's prepare for God's abundant supply in our first steps toward a full heart.

HOLES ON THE SURFACE OF YOUR HEART

Fifteen years in a classroom, teaching reading and writing to seventh graders, gave me plenty of opportunities to enjoy the book, *Holes*. I've read it more times than I can count. Seen the movie too, as a reward for finishing the book, of course. (Teens love a good reward system, especially when it involves a movie.) Maybe that's why the images from the story play with such memorable detail in my mind. Or maybe the images of empty spaces draw me into a place within myself in need of healing by the only One who is able—an all-knowing, loving God who promises to occupy, supply, and spread throughout each and every void.

"The holes look like craters on the moon," one student blurted out as we enjoyed the movie version of the story, and he was right. A bird's-eye view of Camp Green Lake revealed hole after hole covering a vast, brown stretch of wasteland.

Friend, if I could get a glimpse of your heart right now, would it resemble that hole-covered wasteland?

Maybe at this very moment, your "one thing that's missing" feels like it has multiplied. You spend most of your time either thinking of the missing pieces or trying to distract yourself from the constant nagging. Maybe one thing after another has left behind destruction that feels like a minefield of holes. Let me assure you, with all the sincerity in my once-hollow heart, there is hope. God has an ultimate plan to pour into us the full measure of his blessings. And to find out more about each measure, we are inviting Naomi from the Bible along as our guide.

Naomi's heart no doubt matched the crater-filled ground my student described. From her life, we will discover fresh truth we can apply to our own lives today. I am honored and humbled to introduce you to her. As we step back in time and walk alongside this transparent woman of faith, may our hearts remain open to what our Father wants us to receive.

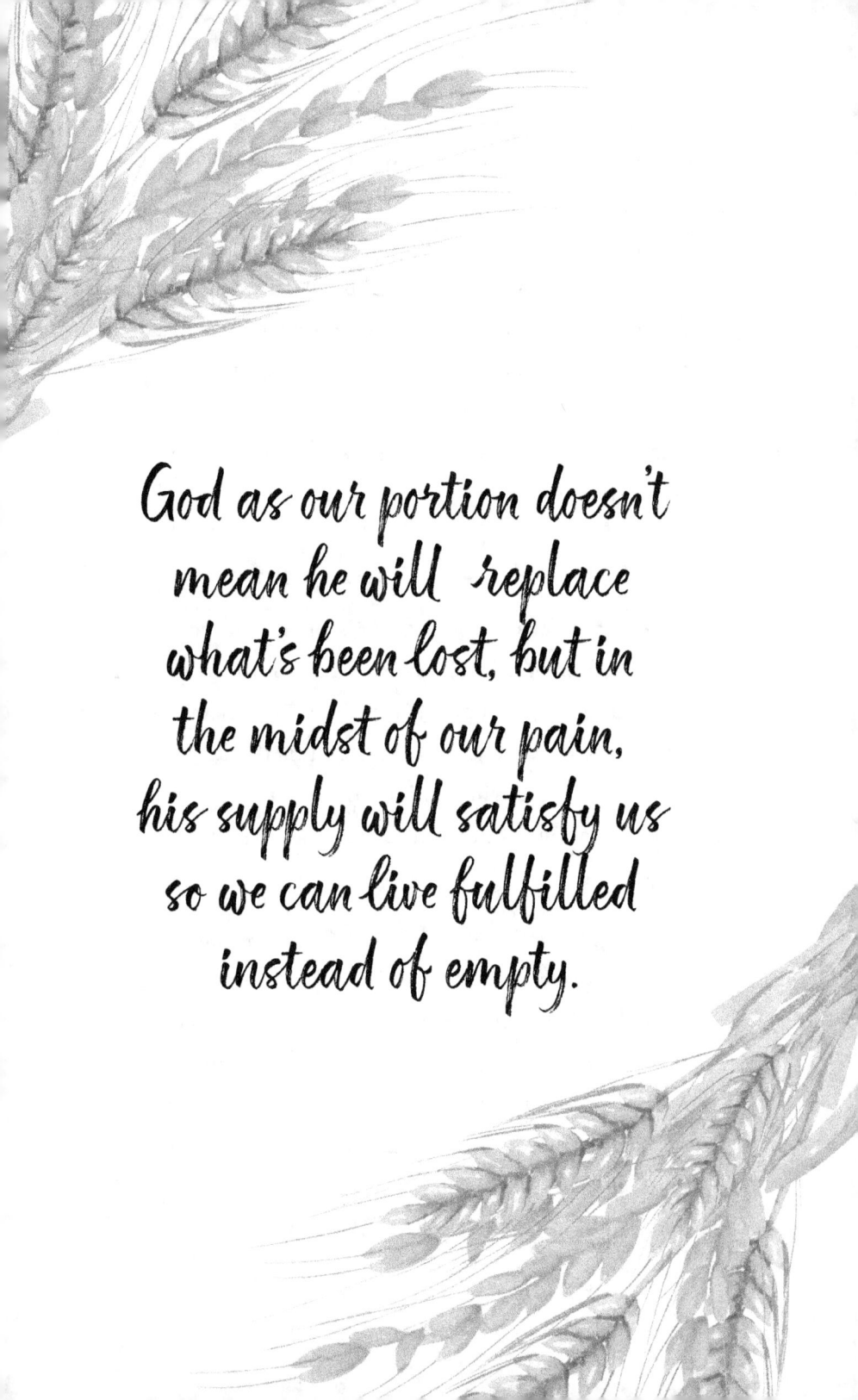

God as our portion doesn't mean he will replace what's been lost, but in the midst of our pain, his supply will satisfy us so we can live fulfilled instead of empty.

In the same way our favorite movie scenes seal in our memories, I believe God will seal our hearts with his truth for our emptiness. To do our part, we will review what we learn in each chapter with statements worth remembering. These short, purposeful thoughts will serve as checkpoints, helping us conclude one leg of our journey before starting the next. We will call them our *measures to remember*. Let's begin with this first measure.

God as our portion doesn't mean he will replace what's been lost, but in the midst of our pain, his supply will satisfy us so we can live fulfilled instead of empty.

OUR HEART-FULL PRAYER

Just like in our favorite books, life is filled with chapters. I've found the most impactful way to transition to the next chapter (both in life and in books) is to close the previous one with prayer. I can't wait for you to get acquainted with Naomi, our woman of the hour. Will you join me for this heart-full prayer before we turn the page on our first chapter together?

Lord,

I've struggled with a void in my life from something I once had that is now gone. The pain is always there as a constant reminder. Thank you for the truth of your Word in Psalm 16:5 that reminds me, "You are my portion and my cup of blessing." Help me learn what it means to live with you as my portion each and every day. You know what I need even before I do. Right now I offer you my empty spaces. I trust you, and I am ready to be refilled. In Jesus' name I pray, Amen.

REFILLED

CHAPTER 2

The Lonely Heart Club

*"and hope does not put us to shame,
because God's love has been poured into our
hearts through the Holy Spirit
who has been given to us"*

ROMANS 5:5

Naomi willed herself to walk out her front door. She stepped across the threshold, whispering one last plea to God before lifting her head and opening her eyes. She hoped the sunrise would reveal a scene of what used to be. Lush vegetation and crops for days. Smiling faces of neighboring women carrying jugs of water without concern for rationing. Kids laughing and playing.

But today it wasn't to be. A barren land stretched out before her.[1] The same discouraging view, for how many days now? She'd lost count. Hard to believe this was the same place God promised his people when he said, "… I have come down to deliver them out of the hand of the Egyptians and to bring them up out of that land to a good and broad land, a land flowing with milk and honey," (Exodus 3:8a).

Was she beginning to question God's promise?

No laughter, no smiles, no harvest. Just deafening silence, the result of the stifled plea of a parched and weary earth. Would she soon hear the cries of her two boys waking, desperate for something to fill their empty bellies? Would she spend another night soothing them to sleep, then praying to the Lord for relief? Their painful cries gnawed at her insides and cut through the quiet.

Truth be told, Naomi and her friends knew this would happen someday. God declared he would allow a famine in the land because of the Israelites' sin. Their not-so-wise ancestors had broken God's commandments, and their disobedience not only led to a lot of wandering in the wilderness,[2] it also created hardships for future generations. God warned them when he said, "I will break your proud spirit by making the skies as unyielding as iron and the earth as hard as bronze. All your work will be for nothing, for your land will yield no crops, and your trees will bear no fruit" (Leviticus 26:19–20 NLT).

Yep, that pretty much summed up their situation.

Maybe that's why her beloved Elimelech mentioned moving to Moab. Surely he couldn't stand to see his wife and boys suffer like this. Maybe he'd convinced himself that his role as the man of the house meant taking control. They depended on their husband and father to care for them. He needed to do something, even as far-fetched as sojourning a while in that God-forsaken place. Maybe, like his precious wife Naomi, the emptiness outside their door matched the hopelessness in his heart.

So they loaded what they had and set out for Moab.

DOING THE WRONG THING FOR ALL THE RIGHT REASONS

"In the days when the judges ruled there was a famine in the land, and a man of Bethlehem in Judah went to sojourn in the country of Moab, he and his wife and his two sons" (Ruth 1:1).

Things may look unfamiliar when we take a step back in time to between 1380–1050 BC and slip into Naomi's sandals.[3] Yet, so much has stayed the same. We've experienced a famine or two, you and me, and famine always causes great turmoil. The sources of our famines may be different, but we find common ground in the pain they inflict. They can also initiate worry over what to do when there seems to be no clear answer.

I, for one, have been guilty of making rash decisions, then rationalizing my wrongdoing, hoping God would forgive me later because it was for the right reasons. This could be why Elimelech took Naomi and their two sons away from their home, community, and everything they knew. I'd like to think his intentions were good.

But hear my heart, dear one. It's important to explore possible reasons why Elimelech and Naomi set out for Moab in the midst of hardship. Motives help us relate to their struggle. We're not here to condemn them for their actions, because we get it. We know the feeling of wanting to trust the Lord in all things but not hearing the answer we seek. We've been there, wanting to do the right thing but ending up doing the wrong thing for the "right" reasons. Our job is not to overanalyze their reasoning or shake our heads in disagreement. Our job is to allow God's Word to saturate our hearts, especially those deep places within us left unkempt for so long. God has a great plan in store for you and me, just as he had for Naomi. Let's seek greater understanding as we continue viewing their circumstances from her perspective.

Naomi lived in a time period in Israel's history when judges ruled. "In those days there was no king in Israel. Everyone did what was right in his own eyes" (Judges 17:6).

That one fact alone speaks volumes about Elimelech's possible frame of mind. Even though we aren't told their thoughts about their move, we do know Elimelech and Naomi would have been aware of God's favor on his chosen people. They would have heard all the stories. How God parted the Red Sea for the Israelites, then closed the waters and drowned the pursuing Egyptian army.[4] How twelve spies brought huge grapes and pomegranates from the Promised Land to show their fellow wanderers what God had in store. How the walls of Jericho fell and how Joshua rescued Rahab and her family from the rubble.[5] Yet, with the knowledge of all those miracles tucked away, they still chose to leave their homeland.

"The name of the man was Elimelech and the name of his wife Naomi, and the names of his two sons were Mahlon and

Chilion. They were Ephrathites from Bethlehem in Judah..." (Ruth 1:2a).

Elimelech's name means "my God is King,"[6] a strong name for a man with an equally strong heritage. The name reveals a profound detail about his life: his upbringing centered on trusting God. In tough times, Elimelech knew the One to turn to, but it's easy to fall into the trap of feeling forgotten by God when daily bread is in short supply.

An Ephrathite was someone who came from Bethlehem Ephrathah, another name for Bethlehem-Judah.[7] Bethlehem means "house of bread." Ephrathah means "fruitful." So, no doubt, this Bethlehem Ephrathah was the place to be![8] The Israelites had been there long enough to put down roots. They had built houses instead of pitching tents, and grown crops and celebrated the harvest. They had lived in the abundance of all God promised.

Elimelech and Naomi weren't the only ones from this fruitful house of bread. One of my other favorite women of faith, Hannah, hailed as an Ephrathite. (She and her husband Elkanah can be read about in 1 Samuel.) But there were even more notable Ephrathites on the way, because the fruitful house of bread had the blessings of God all over it. We will learn more about them as we stick close to Naomi in the pages ahead.

A BAD PLACE TO BE

"They went into the country of Moab and remained there" (Ruth 1:2b).

Naomi and her family trekked across the Jordan River and through the land given to the Israelites of Reuben's clan.[9] They found new dwelling in a country called Moab, just east of the Dead Sea. Moab had plenty, an enticing fact Elimelech found hard to ignore. Each day they'd have more than enough for their family's needs. Everything, that is, except God's blessing.

"It's only temporary," I imagine these two reassured each other. But the temporary refuge also came with temporary fulfillment. The Moabites may have had more, but they had no promises beyond this life, a fact the Israelites knew firsthand. Moab and Israel had been at odds for many years, which made Moab a bad place to be for several compelling reasons.

1. As they camped in the plains of Moab some 250 years prior, before conquering Jericho and claiming the Promised Land, the men of Israel succumbed to the allure of the Moabite women. They fell into immorality and idol worship. "So Israel yoked themselves to the Baal of Peor. And the Lord's anger burned against them" (Numbers 25:3 NIV). As a result, 24,000 of God's people died.[10]

2. Balak, the king of Moab, tried to have a curse put on the Israelites by hiring a man named Balaam. But God wouldn't let that happen. Instead of cursing God's chosen, Balaam spoke these words, "How can I curse whom God has not cursed? How can I denounce whom the Lord has not denounced?" (Numbers 23:8) Balak tried three times to curse them, but God's love for his people remained unchanged (Numbers 24:10).

3. Moab's very existence began in opposition to the goodness of God with Lot's oldest daughter's unfortunate

choice to carry on the family line through her own father.[11] God made his stance on Moab clear when he commanded the Israelites, "Do not seek a treaty of friendship with them as long as you live" (Deuteronomy 23:6 NIV).

I wonder if Elimelech and Naomi considered these things when deciding to sojourn in Moab. Did they create a pros and cons list, adding to each side until confusion caused them to make a judgment call? With all the good reasons they could come up with to leave Bethlehem-Judah, only one reason to have stayed truly mattered.

"For you are a people holy to the Lord your God. The Lord your God has chosen you to be a people for his treasured possession, out of all the peoples who are on the face of the earth" (Deuteronomy 7:6).

Whatever influenced this family's decision to relocate, we can know this. God did not change his mind about choosing them, and he will never change his mind about choosing us. The foundation of God's choice to accept us as his own is something that can never be shaken, will never falter, and will never end. God pointed to us and proclaimed, "Those are my children," because of his steadfast love for us. The next two verses of the above passage in Deuteronomy confirm it.

"It was not because you were more in number than any other people that the Lord set his love on you and chose you, for you were the fewest of all peoples, but it is because the Lord loves you and is keeping the oath that he swore to your fathers..." (Deuteronomy 7:7–8).

I pray we will not miss this, my soul-searching friend. As I write these words, I sense God leading us into a fuller understanding of his love and what that means for our hollow places. God's love can cross borders we never should have crossed, and there is nothing that can stop it. So if we feel far from God, right now we can ditch any lie we've believed for the truth. Nothing can separate us from God's love—an important promise to remember as Naomi took her first steps toward Moab.

"For I am sure that neither death nor life, nor angels nor rulers, nor things present nor things to come, nor powers, nor height nor depth, nor anything else in all creation, will be able to separate us from the love of God in Christ Jesus our Lord" (Romans 8:38–39).

SET APART, OR SEPARATED?

Naomi may have left Bethlehem-Judah because of a famine in the land, but this transition also ushered a famine into her heart.

I can relate to the loneliness Naomi felt as she left her whole life behind. Frequent moves with my husband's job early in our marriage challenged my ability to trust God, embrace newness, and frankly, have a good attitude when I wanted to be somewhere else. Looking back, I can see how God's hand guided us through every difficult move. He gave me plenty of opportunities to persevere and draw closer to him within the transitions, although at the time I didn't see it that way. The loneliness created a void in my heart that refused to be filled.

I remember one particular move that took us farther away from someone we dearly loved. My husband needed the job. He wanted to support his family, and it was a decision unlike any we'd encountered before. We only hoped this was the open door we'd prayed for, and that we'd be able to keep our family relationships strong.

We made the gut-wrenching choice to take the job, even though it meant long stretches of time between visits. I am not going to lie; separation stings. Living apart from someone we love means living each day with a piece missing. And no matter how much we try to avoid the hurt, it's always there.

Being set apart as God's chosen and loved child doesn't make separation any easier. We can love God with every ounce of our being and still experience loneliness. Even with the addition of Facetime and Zoom calls to the world, there are many things that keep us separated.

Like me, maybe a relocation created distance between you and someone you love. Things like military life, kids growing up, or downsizing can lead to living apart. Maybe you've had to find a better place for your aging parent to live, which caused loneliness for the both of you. Or challenges have required you to move to a place where you can get the help you need. If so, then you can relate to what Naomi walked through as she walked away from her friends and neighbors.

Sometimes distance results from a life circumstance, but emotional distance can be just as hard. Strained relationships drive you apart, someone forgets to call, or you feel forgotten by your church family who are supposed to care. So I refuse to take this topic lightly or offer flowery solutions you've heard before, that skim the surface of your hurt. This promise from our heavenly Father will soothe the empty space brought on by separation or loneliness.

God promises to fill us with his love.

"But you, O Lord, are a God merciful and gracious, slow to anger and abounding in steadfast love and faithfulness" (Psalm 86:15).

In her book, *Far From Home*, author Mabel Ninan tells about her experiences as an immigrant, leaving her home in India as a newlywed to move to America. Mabel shared her own struggle with trying to fill her time with activities, jobs, and other things. No matter how hard she tried, her problems in her new life didn't end.

Mabel says, "Deep down, I was aware of a God-shaped hole in my life. I ignored the still voice that kept reminding me that only an intimate relationship with God could fill the void in my soul and offer the right perspective on the changes happening around and within me."[12] She described how transitions can make us feel "less loved and more alienated," but Mabel also offered this hope for those of us who know we're set apart, but need a refresher of God's love, "When we dwell on his steadfast love, his comfort and strength become real and present. His promises give us hope" (Mabel Ninan, *Far From Home*).

FILLED WITH A MEASURE OF GOD'S LOVE

"[A]nd hope does not put us to shame, because God's love has been poured into our hearts through the Holy Spirit who has been given to us" (Romans 5:5).

Did Naomi remember God's love during her time in Moab? Did she ever doubt his love for her when the hole in her heart

God wants to pour his never-ending love into us to soothe the loneliness we feel.

grew? We will explore all this and more as we dig deeper into her life, but first let's bring this chapter to a close with a *measure to remember*.

God wants to pour his never-ending love into us to soothe the loneliness we feel.

When the view in front of us leaves us feeling discouraged, isolated, or even hopeless, this measure to remember assures us of one thing. God will fill us with his love, and there is nothing on earth more plentiful than that.

OUR HEART-FULL PRAYER

Over the course of our time together, we will camp out on ten different things God will use to fill the void in our hearts. The first of these is God's love. Let's pause and pray this heart-full prayer together as we experience his love in full measure.

Dear Lord,

Thank you for your love. It is always with me. Wherever I go or whatever I walk through, I know I can always count on your love to fill me. Romans 5:5 tells me your love is "poured into my heart." So today I am making room for more of your love by giving my hurt and my loneliness to you. At times in my life, I've felt left behind. Separation caused an emptiness I couldn't fill, but you can. Forgive me for letting my emptiness draw me further into despair instead of closer to you. Your love is my portion today, tomorrow, and in the future. In Jesus' name, Amen.

REFILLED

CHAPTER 3

A Little Less Full

"And let the peace of Christ rule in your hearts, to which indeed you were called in one body. And be thankful"

Colossians 3:15

After a busy morning of catching up on long-overdue house cleaning, I sat down on the couch for a coffee break and a few minutes of phone time. I came across an image a friend shared on social media, and the words she added to the post stopped me mid-scroll.

Her image from several years ago showed a group of people, all smiles, gathered in a welcoming outdoor setting. Their casual pose overflowed with love, happiness, and family. I could see it through their expressions, even though I didn't know them. The caption read, "A lot has changed...and our hearts are a little less full."

A little less full. That phrase spoke to my peace-seeking heart. I lingered for a while with the photo my friend posted, holding her memory in the palm of my hand. I couldn't help but wonder who pictured in that image was no longer here. I didn't know the answer, but I could relate to the feeling she so perfectly described. I also have memories on my timeline and in frames on the mantle with missing faces of people pictured who are no longer here—people whose absences left a void, making my life feel a little less full.

Maybe you do, too. Maybe you've struggled with whether to prop that favorite photo of your person on a shelf where you'll pass by it every day or tuck it away in a drawer to keep the hurt from coming back. Not that you'd want to remove their memory, but the hard fact is that the memories, however beautiful, are also painful.

In the days following the death of someone I love, I shut off social media for months, hoping to avoid those reminders popping up on my timeline. I need time to breathe and grieve without the void shouting at me, "A-ha! Here I am again. You can run, but you can't hide from me." I'll wrestle for days over what to do with the memories, how to talk about my person, and how to balance honoring their life and moving forward. It's a fragile walk, and one for which I do not claim to be an expert. Most of the time I'm just fumbling through, letting God help me figure it out little by little.

One thing I do know is this. Eventually, I'm able to look at those precious memories and feel a little less empty. Our hope is that we will get to the place my Facebook friend so sweetly described, where we can share without the fear of grief stealing our peace and contentment for good. We can hope to one day re-

CHAPTER 3 — A LITTLE LESS FULL

share old memories and smile at the thought. I think that's why the particular caption drew me in that day. Over time, we learn to recognize and acknowledge that we're a little less full than we were before. And God is still good.

If, like me, you're still wrestling with how to be at peace in the midst of heartache, this next chapter in Naomi's story will point us toward hope. Let's rejoin our woman of faith in her darkest hour. The next leg of our journey begins there.

ANOTHER HOLE IN NAOMI'S HEART

"What will become of us?"

After another fitful night's sleep, Naomi's first thoughts of the day landed on her beloved Elimelech. Her mind almost tricked her into believing she'd heard his gentle breathing beside her as he roused to begin another day in Moab. But that was just one more hope-killing dream. As her unwanted reality cut through the fog, her next thought turned inward, "How will we make it without him?"

Guilt plagued her over the fact that in her grief, she worried about herself and her boys. "How could I be so selfish?" she likely agonized. Naomi tried to ease up on the hateful self-talk because everyone knew the fate of a widow left behind to care for herself in their cruel world. She knew she should be thankful Mahlon and Chilion had married. Sure, Ruth and Orpah were technically Moabites, but couldn't she still be happy about it? When the boys were young, she didn't know from day to day if they would survive childhood.

As hard as she tried, her rapid-fire thoughts couldn't extinguish the idea that this whole predicament was somehow her fault. If she had known this would happen, they wouldn't have come to Moab in the first place. Guilt, being overwhelmed, and worry gnawed at the pit of grief in Naomi's heart.

"But Elimelech, the husband of Naomi, died, and she was left with her two sons. These took Moabite wives; the name of the one was Orpah and the name of the other Ruth. They lived there about ten years," (Ruth 1:3–4).

The point of view from which I wrote a part of Naomi's story above is fictional, but based on what we know from Scripture. After much time sitting with the Lord about it, I decided those few paragraphs needed sharing. I did not create the fictional scenario about Naomi's thoughts to add to or take away from God's message. I simply want to help us all realize we have much in common when it comes to suffering.

When asked about who Naomi is in the Bible, many of us respond with some reference to her widowhood. We seem to remember her most for what she lost and her bitter attitude about it (which we will talk about in a future chapter). However, we will miss out on a great opportunity if we dismiss her story because we don't think we can relate to her experiences. Even if we cannot identify with someone's circumstances, we stand on common ground through hardship.

CHAPTER 3 — A LITTLE LESS FULL

HOW MUCH CAN ONE PERSON TAKE?

"...and both Mahlon and Chilion died, so that the woman was left without her two sons and her husband" (Ruth 1:5).

Hit with the reality of facing her future without Elimelech, Naomi then experienced every mom's worst nightmare. Her two sons died, adding to the cavernous pit of despair already there. Losing someone we love causes pain beyond words, but the three most important people in her world? The level of grief would be incomprehensible unless we've been there.

As if her pain hadn't piled high enough, now with no one to care for her, hope for the future waned. Just like we discussed with our girl Rahab in *Cinched: Living with Unwavering Trust in an Unfailing God*, in those days "single women and widows were short on choices—an important detail to remember when we're tempted to question what they did to survive."[1] The *Zondervan Illustrated Background Commentary* gives us this reality check, "After her husband's death, normally a widow had to rely on her sons for support; if she had none, she might have to sell herself into slavery, resort to prostitution, or die."

That puts Naomi in a club none of us would ever choose for ourselves or anyone else, with little chance to get out.

Looking at all Naomi lost, we may wonder how much one woman could possibly take before reaching her breaking point. We may also think, "With the voids of so many losses in such a short time, can they ever be refilled?"

I'll bet many of us can nod in solidarity as we ponder those times when everything in life hits at once. During such times, it feels like one bad thing after another, and we cry out to God that we can't take any more. One hole in the heart is bad enough, but then another forms, and another. Soon the number of holes grows to the point we feel like nothingness remains. That's when grief, despair, and hopelessness begin filling the very holes they created. That's also when we must find relief in Jesus. He's our only hope.

Grief comes in many forms. We grieve the death of someone we love. We may also grieve for what might have been. We can grieve over estranged relationships or a loved one's destructive choices. In her heartfelt post, "How Do We Survive Grief for Someone Who Is Still Living," friend and author Abby McDonald shared this thought, "When you love a lost soul, you grieve for the life they could have had."[2] Her words touch a hardened place in my heart where relationships have come and gone, where I've tried to control someone's choices but couldn't, where I sometimes wallow in my own shattered dreams for them.

Grief is so multifaceted, I wouldn't attempt to understand it all or pretend to have the answers. I cannot presume to understand Naomi's grief, although writing this chapter while grieving my own loss made the void much more real. But this one truth I know. The only thing powerful enough to fill the hole left behind by something so hard to understand is the peace that is beyond our understanding.

"Then you will experience God's peace, which exceeds anything we can understand. His peace will guard your hearts and minds as you live in Christ Jesus" (Philippians 4:7 NLT).

CHAPTER 3 — A LITTLE LESS FULL

A PEACE ABOUT IT

In the early days of my faith walk, I wanted to absorb any and all I could from other faith-filled women. I listened. I learned. I focused. I wanted to get as close to Jesus as possible and experience what it meant to "live for Christ." But no matter how much time I spent with my nose in the Bible, I could not get a good strong grip on the idea of *peace*. I wanted it so badly but couldn't figure out how to get it to stick. I prayed, read all the verses, and repeated "do not be anxious about anything" over and over. It helped for a while, but without warning worry and stress would return. I needed the kind of peace that lasts. But how?

I noticed a phrase I'd heard other Christian women say when they would pray and seek God in areas of life where they struggled and decisions had to be made. They'd say, "I have a peace about it." Not just peace, but "a" peace.

Now, to get it right, you need to hear the proper accent as you speak that to yourself. A Texas twang with the emphasis on the word "peace." Then the last two words sort of run together like this: I have a-*peace*-about-it.

I remember the first time I heard that phrase. I thought, "A peace about it? I don't have a peace about anything!" And since I was in the mode of wanting to learn *all* the things, I started on a new quest to discover what it meant to have a peace about every aspect of my life.

A tall order, I know.

If you and I have been connected for a while, either in-person or online, then you've probably already heard me tell about my peace quest. I recall writing about my first encounter with helpful peace-giving verses. I wrote about how I'd been chasing peace, only to realize it was there for the taking all along. In my last book, I shared the story of rediscovering supernatural peace in an MRI tube. I have story after story about moments where peace found me (or where I found peace). Yet here we are, talking about it again, which tells me this desire we have for more peace is not a one-and-done deal, but an ongoing commitment to keep seeking.

As women clawing our way through the unexpected rocky paths of life, we admit we want peace. Most of us would agree we need more of it. Peace is a powerful thing, but I'll be the first to raise my hand and admit trivializing it by tossing the word around so casually. So let's take a step back, look at what God's Word says about it, and get a fresh filling of peace right now.

THE ONLY GIVER OF PERFECT PEACE

John 14 records Jesus speaking to his disciples, who stood at the edge of an uncertain future. Jesus tried to prepare them for his leaving. He tried to explain in ways they could understand. They'd been through the highest highs and the lowest lows with their Savior and Lord, so how could they accept what he now spoke of? The men didn't know what to expect in the next moment, much less the next hour or the next day. They wanted answers and feared the worst, confused by their own consuming thoughts.

In many ways, we can relate to what the disciples experienced as they listened to Jesus' words. What they felt in those hours must have been the opposite of peace! But in the midst of their confusion, Jesus offered them something beyond what this world could ever provide. He gave them the gift of his peace, something he had in abundance. Jesus knew how hard it would be for the disciples to witness what was about to happen to him. The days ahead would test everything he ever taught about the love of the Father, so he spoke this gift into being right before evil set its sinister plan into motion.

"Peace I leave with you; My [perfect] peace I give to you; not as the world gives do I give to you. Do not let your heart be troubled, nor let it be afraid. [Let My perfect peace calm you in every circumstance and give you courage and strength for every challenge]" (John 14:27 AMP).

Through the horrific acts that followed, the disciples watched how Jesus remained peace-filled while enduring unfathomable hurt and betrayal. Jesus gave a priceless gift that day, not just for the disciples, but for each one of us. His peace is the only sure way forward in painful times.

Jesus faced unexplainable pain, and He spoke about peace. By looking at Jesus' example, we can know this. The peace that Jesus offers is the only *perfect* peace. We can talk about peace all day long, but the only way to find perfect peace is through Jesus Christ. All others are just a powerless substitute for the real thing.

The other night, I woke with a start and could not go back to sleep. When this happens, I've learned (the hard way) to have a few go-to verses and worship songs I can call to mind. If I find myself mulling over the events of the day or problems I'm facing, those verses and songs are usually about peace. This particular night, the song "Peace Speaker" began playing on repeat in my thoughts (just the chorus, because that's the part I could remember). I'd heard this old song hundreds of times before. It's a favorite of mine, but these few short lyrics about life's storms supplied me with a fresh revelation that night. "When he (Jesus) says 'peace, be still,' they have to obey." So I hit pause on the song in my thoughts and prayed, "Jesus, speak 'peace, be still' to my mind and heart. Amen." Immediately, my heart calmed, and a feeling of warmth washed over me. I encountered the tangible presence of Jesus' perfect peace.

We talk a lot about God's peace calming the storms in our lives. When storms come in the form of problems, worry, and emotional stress, God will either bring peace to the storm itself or peace to our hearts in the midst of the chaos. I've discovered in my own personal experiences, it's usually the latter. Of course, there are many storms Jesus calms in my life I may never even know about. He's faithful like that.

I've often thought having a moment of peace meant going someplace peaceful like a cabin at the lake or a secluded beach. I love getting away from it all, especially when everything in life hits at once. I want nothing more than to find a place to meet with God and invite his peace into my heart. But have you ever thought about God's peace as so real, so tangible, that it will settle your soul wherever you are and allow you to rest in the middle of wreckage? It is possible, my peace-seeking friend, es-

Peace is not found in a place,
but in the person of Jesus.

pecially when we remember that peace is not found in a place, but in the person of Jesus.

"Now may the Lord of peace himself give you peace at all times in every way. The Lord be with you all" (2 Thessalonians 3:16).

So for this chapter's *measure to remember*, I'd like for us to take this thought to heart as a soothing balm for any grief, despair, or loss we experience. This truth has had such a profound impact on my peace-seeking journey, it bears repeating. Our next measure to remember is this: Peace is not found in a place, but in the person of Jesus.

FILLED WITH A MEASURE OF GOD'S PEACE

Seeking peace may come easier in the context of a busy season or decisions that must be made, but we can't forget the level of hardship our friend Naomi faced—her grief, despair, and loss. Is Jesus' perfect peace powerful enough to fill the emptiness Naomi felt? Let's look to one final verse from God's Holy Word for the answer to that question.

"May the God of hope fill you with all joy and peace in believing, so that by the power of the Holy Spirit you may abound in hope" (Romans 15:13).

Yes, sweet sister, God planned to fill Naomi with the perfect peace that would one day carry his only Son through the pain of the cross. And that same peace is available to us right now. Astonishing, isn't it? We don't have to chase it down or follow some formula to get it. We only need to spend more time with the Peace Speaker. Then we can know that in times when our hearts are a little less full, because of Jesus, we can still smile.

OUR HEART-FULL PRAYER

In this chapter we set up camp together around our shared experiences in times of grief. We learned that God can and will fill us with peace. Let's pray this heart-full prayer and ask for Jesus' perfect peace to saturate our minds and hearts.

Dear Jesus,

Thank you for your gift of peace. The peace the world gives will never satisfy, but you offer perfect peace that will change my life. Romans 15:13 tells me that you will fill me with perfect peace. Philippians 4:7 tells me your peace, which surpasses understanding, will guard my heart and mind. In my hardest days, in times of great loss, and in my deepest suffering, your presence will bring a level of peace beyond anything I can create on my own. Thank you, Jesus. Speak peace, be still, to my mind and heart. In your name I pray, Amen.

REFILLED

CHAPTER 4

An Omer of Good Things

*"For he satisfies the thirsty and fills
the hungry with good things"*

PSALM 107:9 NLT

Naomi and her two daughters-in-law lived a reality determined to teach them a rock-hard lesson, like dry earth without an ounce of refreshment. Their list of tragedies added up to limited options.

Naomi might've mulled over their situation, although in Scripture's account, it appears the decision came the instant she heard news from back home. How long she considered what to do, we don't know, but we do know what they were likely to face.

Reality number one: their supply would soon run out. Reality number two: they had no means to get more. Reality number three: even if they did find a way to survive, people with bad intentions had a sneaky way of sniffing out unassuming widows in their distress. Even the most courageous woman would shudder at the thought of that third reality.

Yet, a new truth beckoned Naomi.

"Then Naomi heard in Moab that the Lord had blessed his people in Judah by giving them good crops again" (Ruth 1:6 NLT).

This resourceful lady somehow came upon good news in the fields of Moab. The news she heard restored a glimmer of hope. God had blessed his people in Bethlehem with provision. Back across the Dead Sea, the Israelites enjoyed life-giving food.

A sweet, sweet blessing indeed.

Armed with this new bucketful of information, Naomi decided to pack what wouldn't weigh them down and head back home. "Her decision to return to Bethlehem was the most reasonable option; there she might at least find sustenance by gleaning if no extended family members were to care for her."[1] As she knew from past experience, this journey wouldn't be easy. It would take perseverance, fortitude, and a lot of prayer for protection along the way—all things she had in short supply.

So what propelled Naomi toward home? Maybe she chose to think about what she *did* have: knowledge of the power of her Almighty God who'd done great things for his chosen children. This points us back to one thing we gleaned just two short chapters ago. God's goodness to his people never expires.

Some 500 years later, a psalmist would write lyrics expressing this promise. "For it was I, the Lord your God, who rescued you from the land of Egypt. Open your mouth wide, and I will *fill it with good things*" (Psalm 81:10 NLT, Emphasis mine).

CHAPTER 4 — AN OMER OF GOOD THINGS

God's goodness to his people fueled Naomi as she planned her trip back to Bethlehem-Judah. Faith awaited her return.

EMPTY-SHELF TIMES

Let's take a minute to pause and think of a desperate time in our lives when we didn't have what we needed to survive—a time when we opened the cabinet or pantry and saw nothing inside. Whether a literal cabinet or a figurative one representing something we can't see or touch, an empty shelf is a scary thing. Much like the drought-filled days when Naomi opened her front door to nothingness, the emptiness of our shelves resembles the desert-stricken land she once knew.

Even if we have a willingness to do whatever it takes to fill the shelves, we often don't know how or when the answer will come. We have no clue what will happen to us.

I recall not too long ago seeing a group of young mothers experiencing an empty-shelf time of their own. Anxious posts from moms in search of infant formula filled my social media newsfeed. Vacant store shelves replaced the once-stocked products. I could feel the desperation in their hearts as they reached out asking loved ones to keep an eye open at their local stores for the food their babies needed. Words like "product unavailable" and "out of stock" added to their discouragement.

How do we know God will supply if all we see is emptiness around us?

When what we need gets stripped away and we suddenly don't know what to do, we look ahead and agonize over where provision will come from and when the answer will arrive.

Stress, panic, and frustration fill our hearts so we have no room left. We question whether there's enough in reserve to make it through until next year, next month, or maybe even next week. And if we're honest, we question why God doesn't restock the shelves.

Uncertainty can shake our faith. Yet, it's in those desolate times God gives us the opportunity to grow that faith. Without our empty-shelf moments, we wouldn't see God's great plan for providing in every area of our lives.

That's easier to say, now that I can look back and see how God sustained me through the most difficult times. But what about when we're neck deep in the middle of the distress? How do we demonstrate lasting faith when we fear we don't have enough to get beyond today? Let's look to another brave woman in the Bible for what to do when the shelves are empty.

THE WIDOW OF ZAREPHATH'S ALMOST-EMPTY SHELVES

Like Naomi, another widow in Scripture understood the pain of living empty. We know her only by her location, not by her name. We also know her circumstances had progressed from bad to worse. Let's walk with her through her story.

Gathering sticks near the town gate, her thoughts fixated on her predicament. If there was ever a time to entertain strangers, this was not it. A man approached her before she could avoid eye contact and rush off in the opposite direction. She had more pressing worries than to get sidetracked by someone she didn't even know.

CHAPTER 4 — AN OMER OF GOOD THINGS

"So he went to Zarephath. As he arrived at the gates of the village, he saw a widow gathering sticks, and he asked her, 'Would you please bring me a little water in a cup?' As she was going to get it, he called to her, 'Bring me a bite of bread, too'" (1 Kings 17:10–11 NLT).

The widow couldn't deal with that at the time. She'd done the best she could in the drought. Her ability to provide for her and her son quickly faded, along with the hope of any future for them both. Her polite refusal would have to do.

"And she said, 'As the Lord your God lives, I have nothing baked, only a handful of flour in a jar and a little oil in a jug. And now I am gathering a couple of sticks that I may go in and prepare it for myself and my son, that we may eat it and die'" (1 Kings 17:12).

Contrary to the manners of the day, this man named Elijah wouldn't take no for an answer. This sparked a shocking turn of events for a woman with more pressing issues on her mind.

"And Elijah said to her, 'Do not fear; go and do as you have said. But first make me a little cake of it and bring it to me, and afterward make something for yourself and your son'" (1 Kings 17:13).

In the very next verse, the prophet Elijah told her everything she needed to know about trusting God for provision, "For thus says the Lord, the God of Israel, 'The jar of flour shall not be spent, and the jug of oil shall not be empty, until the day that the Lord sends rain upon the earth.'"

There she was, ready to die. Her words revealed the resolve in her heart. Whatever happened, she had to release control and trust the outcome to God. Only, the outcome looked bleak from where she stood. Her faithfulness to a God she loved still guided her decisions through her lack. She chose to obey the man of God and give out of her meager means.

The widow's story is so profound; I don't want us to rush past this lesson too quickly. She looked ahead and thought about her future. At first, she made assumptions based on the one measly serving left in her jar. Then, she remembered to rely on God for it.

In the depth of emptiness, hopelessness finds opportunity. And hopelessness wants us to believe the lie that God doesn't have enough miracles for what we need. The widow's story refutes that lie with the simplicity of God's character. We serve a faithful God, and all we need to bring to the table is enough faith for the moment.

"And she went and did as Elijah said. And she and he and her household ate for many days. The jar of flour was not spent, neither did the jug of oil become empty, according to the word of the Lord that he spoke by Elijah" (1 Kings 17:15–16).

GOD'S MEASUREMENT INSTEAD OF THE WORLD'S

God gave the widow of Zarephath exactly what she needed for the day's meal. When that was gone, he filled her jar again for the next. This brings to mind a question we need to ask ourselves at this stop on our journey.

Are we satisfied with God's blessing for today, or do we feel disappointed when we don't have an abundance?

CHAPTER 4 — AN OMER OF GOOD THINGS

The widow of Zarephath's jug was almost empty. Only a few drops remained. Often in my circumstances, I've stored up extras but still questioned if God would come through. I've wrung my hands and fretted about my needs long before the need became desperate. That's why noticing how God responded to the widow's lack is so important. God provided when merely a drop of oil remained, and he did so by giving one day's serving at a time.

In my study of Naomi's life, I came across an eye-opening description of how the Israelites measured wheat, barley, and other dry goods in their day. We will discover the divine significance of barley in chapter eight. For now, let's look to these original Hebrew measurements for new insight on a powerful promise from our Almighty God.

An *omer* refers to a unit of measurement that equals about two quarts. That would be an accurate measurement if someone, say, gave you a few scoops of grain to carry home. Multiply that amount times ten, and you have an *ephah*. An ephah of grain would be roughly twenty quarts or three-fifths of a bushel. (Here's where it gets exciting.) Add ten ephahs together, and you get a *homer*. That's over six bushels full...not a gift you'd be able to carry on your own. You'd need a good, strong donkey to help you haul it all.[2]

So, if we think of these measurements in light of our question above, we get a clearer idea of the balance between God's plan for provision and his measureless abundance. When we pray, we do so knowing God is capable of pouring out an ephah or even a homer of good things, and sometimes he does. Other times, God provides only what we need to sustain us, so we will keep trusting him for each day's omer.

With that in mind, our question should become, "Will I trust God for provision for right now, while also trusting him for everything beyond today?" Each *omer* from God adds to the one before, ensuring we have what we need. Before we know it, we can look back and see the *homer* of goodness God provided throughout our lives.

Something to think about as we watch Naomi, Ruth, and Orpah venture with few possessions into an unknown future.

WHEN WHAT WE NEED CAN'T SIT ON A SHELF

Taking a stroll around the yard has always ranked at the top of my favorite things to do. I hadn't enjoyed the outdoors in a while, since doctors advised against any prolonged sun exposure. At the time that didn't matter, though, because getting out of bed felt like climbing a mountain.

Nearing the end of the last round of radiation and chemotherapy, I stepped out into the backyard for the first time in weeks and turned my face toward the sun. The warmth of the morning rays soothed my soul in ways I cannot describe. I still moved like a snail, shuffling along in my bathrobe and slippers. I had a long way to go toward healing, but that day gave me hope.

I paused, chin up like a sundial, and thought about each day of treatment. When I began, I saw this mountainous obstacle positioned in front of me. It seemed too scary and too impossible to reach the other side. By default, I could only focus on

God will give us
what we need for today,
and that is enough.

strength enough for one day at a time. I may have ended each day exhausted, wondering if tomorrow would be better, but I also thanked God for giving me what I needed for one more day.

Provision comes in many forms, which may be why I love the opening verse for this chapter where the psalmist wrote how God "fills the hungry with good things" (Psalm 107:9). The ESV offers an even deeper insight into God's unending supply.

"For he satisfies the longing soul, and the hungry soul he fills with good things."

The words *longing soul* stir something inside, like God gave the writer that inspiration for me alone. I know it's not just for me, however, because we are all longing souls in need of sustenance. Like he did for the widow of Zarephath, God will supply the food and shelter we need to live. God also provides in many other unexpected ways.

He calms our anxious thoughts and eases our fears. He lifts our spirits with the words of Scripture and encourages us to smile again. He gives us energy to get out of bed and peace through difficult situations. He brings a friend to our side with a text or call at just the right time and nudges us to do the same for someone else. He stirs our hearts to make a meal for a struggling neighbor. He restores what we've lost. He renews our hope. I could go on, but I believe you're adding your own promises to the list, as well. So let me close my personal story with our *measure to remember*: God will give us what we need for today, and that is enough.

Let's take a moment to commit this thought to memory as we thank God for the good things he provides.

CHAPTER 4 — AN OMER OF GOOD THINGS

FILLED WITH A MEASURE OF GOOD THINGS

In this chapter, we discovered how God will fill us with good things. Psalm 103 also expresses God's goodness with this holy proclamation, "He fills my life with good things. My youth is renewed like the eagle's!" (Psalm 103:5 NLT).

The psalmist David spells out a few of those good things in the two preceding verses, "He forgives all my sins and heals all my diseases. He redeems me from death and crowns me with love and tender mercies" (Psalm 103:3–4 NLT).

He forgives. Heals. Redeems. Crowns.

For the widow of Zarephath, God's *good things* meant the provision for one meal at a time. For Naomi, provision waited on the other side of a life-threatening trip across land that held unpredictable hurdles. With the hope of home refilling her spirit, Naomi made the choice to go.

"So she set out from the place where she was with her two daughters-in-law, and they went on the way to return to the land of Judah" (Ruth 1:7).

The New Living Translation puts it this way, "…they took the road that would lead them back to Judah."

Was Naomi seeking forgiveness, healing, redemption, a crown of love and tender mercies? What might she discover, besides food to fill the hunger inside? Many times our emptiness expands so deep and wide we don't even know what we seek. Its bigness is daunting and honestly, we struggle to believe God is bigger.

So I say this prayerfully and with great care for what you may be going through at this moment. Whatever you need to fill your longing soul, my sister, God has a precise measure ready to pour at the right time, and it is more than enough. Let's pack up this chapter by crying out to our Great Provider with a heart-full prayer. Let's open our longing souls and trust him to fill us with good things.

OUR HEART-FULL PRAYER

As we reflect on times in our own lives when God provided, let's go to him in prayer with an attitude of thanksgiving. Like the psalmist who praised God for the good things in his life, we, too, can praise him for his faithfulness while trusting him to fill the empty shelves of our lives and hearts.

Dear God,

Thank you for filling my life with good things. You are faithful, loving, and merciful. I praise you for who you are. I believe you will provide for my every need. Thank you for your promise to fill me in full measure. The words of Psalm 107:9 are the cry of my longing soul, because I know you "satisfy the thirsty and fill the hungry with good things." Opening the cabinet and seeing empty shelves can be frightening, but those are the times you beckon me to trust you more. When emptiness looms large and I can't see a means for provision, send your help. My faith is in you. In Jesus' name I pray, Amen.

REFILLED

CHAPTER 5

Give Me Strength!

*"My flesh and my heart may fail,
but God is the strength of my heart
and my portion forever"*

PSALM 73:26

Three heartbroken women set out on a days-long trek across dangerous terrain.[1] Mental and emotional strain from the grief they shared took a toll long before the physical exertion even began. In their weary state, would they make it to Bethlehem-Judah? Would they have the strength they needed for the road ahead? The women hadn't ventured far before Naomi's exhaustion came to the surface and revealed itself in a shocking decision. "But Naomi said to her two daughters-in-law, 'Go, return each of you to her mother's house. May the Lord deal kindly with you, as you have dealt with the dead and with me'" (Ruth 1:8).

Naomi wanted Ruth and Orpah to turn back and settle in Moab. It might appear at first glance that selfishness motivated

Naomi's decision, but that wasn't the case, as we can see from her following comment.

"'The Lord grant that you may find rest, each of you in the house of her husband!' Then she kissed them, and they lifted up their voices and wept" (Ruth 1:9).

Naomi cared for her two daughters-in-love. She'd taken a treacherous journey to a distant land before, when her late husband Elimelech brought them to Moab in the first place. She knew the challenges they'd encounter, and she didn't want that for her girls.

Naomi wanted Ruth and Orpah to find rest. Not the kind of rest we might enjoy when our toddler takes an extended afternoon nap, or when daylight saving time hits and we get an extra hour of sleep. This rest Naomi mentioned went beyond that. The Hebrew word for rest Naomi used in this passage means "a resting place, rest, or comfortable."[2] She desired they get the rest like God promised his people before they set foot across the Jordan River for the first time, "for you have not as yet come to *the rest* and to the inheritance that the LORD your God is giving you" (Deuteronomy 12:9).

Naomi wanted more for her sons' widows than the life she could give them. She wanted them to have a life where they could be provided for by faithful husbands, free from past worries and struggles. They deserved that, after what they'd endured at their young ages. If she had to live a life marred by tragedy, at least Ruth and Orpah could find some semblance of normalcy with new husbands and have their needs met. That was the best-case scenario Naomi could dream up for them, but would this kind of rest be possible in Moab?

A BETTER KIND OF REST

"And they said to her, 'No, we will return with you to your people.' But Naomi said, 'Turn back, my daughters; why will you go with me? Have I yet sons in my womb that they may become your husbands? Turn back, my daughters; go your way, for I am too old to have a husband. If I should say I have hope, even if I should have a husband this night and should bear sons, would you therefore wait till they were grown? Would you therefore refrain from marrying? No, my daughters, for it is exceedingly bitter to me for your sake that the hand of the Lord has gone out against me'" (Ruth 1:10–13).

Naomi's response demonstrated how she felt—physically tired, emotionally depleted, and mentally spent.

Naomi spilled her thoughts in hopes that her explanation would make sense to Ruth and Orpah. In Naomi's mind, the young women stood a better chance at a restful life by returning to their families in Moab than accompanying her to her homeland.[3]

I can totally relate to this part in Naomi's story. She'd thought this whole thing through more than once, growing wearier by the day. She looked ahead at every possibility and decided on the path of least resistance for her girls. Although Naomi should have known more than most, there is no such thing as playing it safe for a child of God. We do our best to put our lives in our Creator's outstretched hands and leave the future to him. Like Naomi, however, we can let our difficult circumstances deceive us into believing it's all up to us to find the right solution.

Trusting God with our lives and the lives of our loved ones takes practice. We explored this as we walked alongside Rahab in the book *Cinched*. We learned how cinching our rope represents tying our hope to his outcomes, not our own.[4] Yet our minds are so complex, so intricate, we can think of endless paths from which to choose. Then, we mistake "choosing a certain path" for following God's plan. We convince ourselves that the outcome depends on us, and if we choose wrong, we will thwart God's ultimate plan for our lives. Thankfully, when we release control to the Author of our story, we cannot mess up the beautiful plan he scripted for us.

"A man's mind plans his way [as he journeys through life], But the Lord directs his steps *and* establishes them" (Proverbs 16:9 AMP).

I've been in Naomi's sandals, overthinking my situation and feeling the effects of mental exhaustion. I've tried to make an important decision and gotten frustrated when my loved ones wouldn't comply. I've wanted "what's best" for them. I've plotted out the most viable possibilities and made a choice based on a plausible outcome. Like Naomi, in my weariness, I've forgotten how God's outcome is always far better than what I can think or imagine. I only need to trust him with it, because he has a better kind of rest available.

MENTALLY SPENT

Waking up, I clicked my phone to see the word *Monday* on the screen. *How could it be time to wake up already?* I wondered why I felt too tired to function, when I hadn't done anything to exert myself all weekend long. I dragged myself out of bed, hoping an extra cup of coffee would wash away the fatigue.

I didn't realize I'd spent so much mental energy over the weekend thinking about all the problems that needed solving. I'd convinced myself the problems were mine to solve. Soon, more problems emerged. The crazy thing about problems is how they tend to multiply in our minds. One issue opens the door to another, then another. Soon I found myself buried under the weight of issues God never meant for me to lift. As a result, I started my week completely spent.

Our overworked minds can weaken us, even if we haven't been physically active. It has recently been proven that mental fatigue can affect our perceived physical fatigue.[5] That feeling of exhaustion at the end of the day when you weren't doing much? It's real. And like me, maybe your brain has been working overtime again.

Ever have one of those days when your brain just will not shut off? And the harder you try to relax, the worse the tension gets? My mind seems stuck in overdrive most days, and I'm always looking for ways to slow it down. The effects of a weary mind can be devastating to our lives. Thankfully, God's Word gives us hope-filled truth about God's design for rest that we can apply to our minds.

In chapter 33 of Exodus, God commanded Moses to leave Sinai and move his people toward the land he promised to give them. God even said he would drive out enemies before them. But then, God informed Moses he would not be going along, since the people had been rebellious and stubborn.

"Go up to a land flowing with milk and honey; but I will not go up among you, lest I consume you on the way, for you are a stiff-necked people" (Exodus 33:3).

Moses didn't want to go anywhere without God, so he sought the Lord on behalf of the Israelites. Moses prayed, "... please show me now your ways" (Exodus 33:13). Moses interceded for the people, and God responded with a promise of his presence and *rest*.

"And He said, 'My presence will go with you, and I will give you rest'" (Exodus 33:14).

Moses knew in order to fully understand God's ways, we must invite him to go with us. There's nothing quite like the feeling of knowing God is with us. I love how God reassured Moses he would find rest from worry while in God's presence. The NLT version puts it this way, "I will personally go with you, Moses, and I will give you rest—everything will be fine for you."

What a refreshing promise from the Lord! Moses discovered a valuable truth about God's character that day, and through this story in Exodus, we can let it bring relief to our minds, as well.

God's rest is a rest that lasts a lifetime.

God doesn't want his daughters buried under the weight of overwhelming thoughts. He wants us to rest, knowing he is with us. Imagine right now God speaking that same word to us that he spoke to Moses. "Everything will be fine for you. I'm here. You can rest."

That's our promise for our overworked minds. The next time we wake up with a weariness we can't seem to shake (even with that extra cup of morning coffee) let's remember the promise. God's rest can only be discovered while lying down in green pastures and following him beside still waters (Psalm 23:2). May we understand that his rest is the only kind that truly lasts a lifetime.

PHYSICALLY TIRED

In our last chapter, we glimpsed at a time in my life when physical pain and tiredness were my constant companions. The result of weeks of cancer treatments pulverized my body, inside and out. When I awoke, pain and tiredness were there. When I tried to walk to the mailbox or into the backyard for a bit of sunshine, they came with me. When I retreated to bed at night and prayed the next day I'd feel better, pain and tiredness crawled into bed beside me, nagging, poking, and prodding until I'd finally take something prescribed by the doctor just to have a moment of relief.

As I shared more about my cancer battle with my faithful community of subscribers at kristinebrown.net, many of you responded with your own stories of chronic illness. I read of your experiences with daily pain and issues that kept you from doing the things in life that truly mattered to you. I realized I wasn't alone in my suffering, and many of us live with a void created by physical pain and conditions beyond our control. Each day we try to deal with what we cannot do and question if we will ever get better.

I've heard it said, "If we're still here, then God still has a purpose for us." I can't say for certain where that catchy phrase originated, but when my body is wrecked with pain, I don't need catchy phrases or trite comments. I need something substantial to not only strengthen my weary body, but also to ease the void that screams, "You're of no use to anyone anymore!" The only thing powerful enough to do both those things is the strength poured into us by the Original Source of all strength.

I met writer and YouTube channel host, Judy Sheer Watters, through a mutual writing friend. Judy and I recorded a conversation for her YouTube channel, "You Have a Story to Tell." While watching one of her episodes as I prepared to record, I related to a difficult time Judy was walking through in her own life. I felt compelled to share that piece of her story with you here, and Judy has graciously given me permission to do so.

You see, Judy had been dealing with health issues, which led to an unexpected hiatus from recording videos for her channel. She had to step away from the ministry she felt called to do. During her extended break, she endured one physical setback after another. Because of the pain, she could not care for her grandchild the way she wanted to. Sadness set in. Physical challenges took their toll, not only fueling the pain, but also affecting other areas of her daily life. Her social calendar had once been full, but now those fun things were replaced with doctor's appointments. (Oh, how I can relate!)

Listening to Judy tell of her struggle, her smile spoke volumes about her outlook. Even as she acknowledged the difficulties, she looked for something positive to focus on. Judy chose to find good in the midst of the struggle, which I know firsthand is hard to do. In talking about her relationship with her grandchild, Judy's face glowed. She shared how even though they couldn't have their usual weekly visits, Judy would soon start pool exercises at her granddaughter's house, giving her the opportunity to spend time with her. Judy found something to cherish amid all her health issues. She offered this encouragement, which I need to heed in my own life, as well. "In our downturns, we need to look at the bright side."[6]

Maybe, like the personal struggle I shared, you are in a place where chronic pain or health issues chip away at a void in your heart. And in your weakened state, you wonder if God still has a purpose for you. You long for what once was and are unable to see that things will ever be like they were. If that describes you, my faithful friend, then maybe you don't want me to tell you to "look at the bright side." But trust me with this.

Let's pause and think of the brightness as Jesus himself, warming our hearts and easing our hurt. Finding a positive place for our focus may seem impossible, but with God's strength and a bit of resolve, we can. We will dig deeper into the Light of Jesus in a later chapter, but I felt compelled to bring it up here as we search for a little brightness where chronic illness resides.

May we all let Judy's wise words settle into our spirits when affliction takes its toll. Physical challenges can weaken our bodies, but we can choose to find the brightness to illuminate our hearts in the midst of the pain.

EMOTIONALLY DEPLETED

"Then they lifted up their voices and wept again. And Orpah kissed her mother-in-law, but Ruth clung to her. And she said, 'See, your sister-in-law has gone back to her people and to her gods; return after your sister-in-law'" (Ruth 1:14–15).

Emotions ran high as the grieving widows hugged for what might be the last time. With tears flowing, Naomi refused to take no for an answer. She'd managed to convince Orpah, but Ruth's stubbornness would not quit. Naomi gave it one last try by pointing out again how Ruth would be better off following her sister-in-law's lead.

But Ruth had made up her mind, and nothing Naomi said would change it.

"But Ruth said, 'Do not urge me to leave you or to return from following you. For where you go I will go, and where you lodge I will lodge. Your people shall be my people, and your God my God. Where you die I will die, and there will I be buried. May the Lord do so to me and more also if anything but death parts me from you.' And when Naomi saw that she was determined to go with her, *she said no more*" (Ruth 1:16–18, Emphasis mine).

I can't help being inspired by Ruth's resolve in her words spoken to Naomi. It's a declaration of loyalty and commitment rarely seen between women in Scripture. With the powerful message in Ruth's plea, I don't want us to miss the last sentence of verse eighteen, where the perspective shifts to our girl, Naomi. It also signals a shift in Naomi's state of being: "And when Naomi saw that she (Ruth) was determined to go with her, she said no more."

Naomi didn't have the capacity to keep fighting. She waved the white flag. I imagine her throwing her hands up in surrender and thinking, "I give up!" She'd been pushed to the limits of what she could handle mentally, physically, and emotionally. She saw Ruth's determination and realized it was time to concede, which is exactly what she needed to do.

Naomi recognized her own capacity. This brings up an important question as we take a closer look inside our own empty spaces and see what resides there. Are we pushing forward in our own strength? Taking on a heavier load than God intended for us to carry? Maybe we started with the best intentions to invite God to be present in our suffering and to fill us with what we needed to get through each day. Then, without realizing it, we shifted into doing things in our own strength. We gave in as our minds, bodies, and emotions started running the show, leaving us depleted and ready to throw our hands up in a signal of defeat.

If these words describe you, my load-bearing friend, I'm right there with you. Let's take our cue from Naomi and recognize our limited capacity for handling all the things! We discovered early in this chapter how God blesses us with the gift of true rest. Now, let's accept his blessing of strength. When we're worn out to the point of weary, we find strength in God. Just hear these words from the prophet Isaiah, "Do you not know? Have you not heard? The Lord is the everlasting God, the Creator of the ends of the earth. He will not grow tired or weary, and his understanding no one can fathom. He gives strength to the weary and increases the power of the weak" (Isaiah 40:28–29 NIV).

Chronic illness is only one of many things that can cause pain and exhaustion in our lives, leaving us void of the strength we once had. Maybe you are not the one in physical pain, but you've been called on to take care of someone who is. Caregiving for a loved one with a debilitating condition takes weariness to a whole different level. Or maybe you've given your time to raising

God never grows tired or weary. He is ready to fill us with the strength to carry us through whatever we face.

a grandchild. You feel a love for this child greater than anything you've ever known, yet you also reminisce over the retirement years you gave up for this unexpected purpose.

Whether managing our own health issues, caring for others, or being overwhelmed beyond our capacity, we can know this: we may grow tired and weary, but God never will. Let's get ready for a refilling of God's strength today.

FILLED WITH A MEASURE OF GOD'S STRENGTH

"I pray that from his glorious, unlimited resources he will empower you with inner strength through his Spirit" (Ephesians 3:16 NLT).

Naomi and Ruth would need God's strength to make the journey to Bethlehem-Judah. Even on a good day, two women stood a slim chance of making it there safely. These two women—tired, depleted, and spent—had about as much chance as a wounded animal wandering through predator territory. But they also had something no enemy could steal…power and protection from the One who never grows tired or weary, ready to fill them with a measure of strength to carry them home. Let's close with that thought as our *measure to remember*.

God never grows tired or weary. He is ready to fill us with the strength to carry us through whatever we face.

OUR HEART-FULL PRAYER

Through the intense conversation between Naomi, Ruth, and Orpah, we learned how we often rely on our own strength to face the challenges ahead. When our supply is depleted, we can turn to God and trust him to strengthen our weary hearts. We've unearthed how God will fill us with love, peace, and good things. Now, we can add strength to our growing list. Let's pray for a fresh filling of God's strength.

Dear God,

I am weary. I have overestimated my capacity and tried to find relief in my own strength. I lift my hands in surrender, Lord. I ask you to fill my cup with your strength. I cannot do this without you. Thank you for being a God who never grows tired or weary. Thank you for the strength to ease my physical pain as well as my emotional and mental exhaustion. Thank you for helping me recognize my capacity and for providing true rest. Your Word says in Psalm 73:26, "My flesh and my heart may fail, but God is the strength of my heart and my portion forever." I praise you for being my portion to fill the void left by weariness. In Jesus' name, Amen.

REFILLED

CHAPTER 6

Bitter Woman

"See to it that no one fails to obtain the grace of God; that no "root of bitterness" springs up and causes trouble, and by it many become defiled"

HEBREWS 12:15

"So the two of them went on until they came to Bethlehem. And when they came to Bethlehem, the whole town was stirred because of them. And the women said, 'Is this Naomi?'" (Ruth 1:19).

Naomi had been away from her homeland for years. Her people expressed great enthusiasm over her homecoming. The New Living Translation tells us, "... the entire town was excited by their arrival." I can picture the hullabaloo now. Friends wanted to hear all about her life in Moab. Besties she hadn't seen in ages pushed to the front of the pack, ready to hug her neck. Former neighbors strained to see her, speculating about her two boys and wondering about the young travel mate they spotted arriving with her.

Reunions can be fun and overwhelming, all at the same time. Sometimes we just want to slip in unnoticed, without all the fanfare. Other times we can't wait to reunite and catch up on things with our people. With the atmosphere of excitement surrounding Naomi's return, imagine their shock at her confession in the next breath.

"She said to them, 'Do not call me Naomi; call me Mara, for the Almighty has dealt very bitterly with me. I went away full, and the Lord has brought me back empty. Why call me Naomi, when the Lord has testified against me and the Almighty has brought calamity upon me?'" (Ruth 1:20–21).

The name *Naomi* means "my joy." The name *Mara* means "bitter."[1] Naomi returned to Bethlehem a bitter woman.

Bitterness. It's something we've all experienced but don't like to admit. We'd rather hide it in our heart than let others know we're struggling with it. Shame keeps us from reaching out for help because we worry what others might think. So as women who believe in the power of God and his forgiveness, why do we battle bitterness?

Bitterness gives us a temporary feeling of satisfaction. Thinking about the hurtful things we've endured, we can convince ourselves the bitterness is justified, but here's the thing. Entertaining bitter feelings never provides lasting relief. It blocks the healing and peace our souls desperately need.

The *Oxford Dictionary* defines bitterness as "anger and disappointment at being treated unfairly; resentment." I, for one, have been stung by bitterness, letting it work its way into my heart and mind. I've fought against it time and time again, and have seen the damage it causes. Confessing my own bout with bitterness has taken a level of courage I haven't tapped into before, so I pray you'll be patient with me as we dig into this chapter. I believe it's a critical piece of Naomi's story, and of ours, as well. And we know from past experiences, sometimes the greatest healing comes from the hardest places.

Naomi's declaration showed the condition of her heart. The bitterness she harbored had turned Naomi into a different person. Let's take a deeper look at why Naomi resorted to such a self-condemning statement. New growth waits for us on the other side as we learn from her example. Let's begin to break up dry earth and explore what the Bible says about bitterness and how to get rid of it for good.

WHO ARE YOU?

Recently, bitterness over years of past hurts bubbled to the surface of my heart. I thought I had dealt with it. I thought I'd learned to "let it go." But then the anger and frustration triggered it again. I rehearsed Isaiah 26:3 to keep bitterness from gaining ground, "You keep him in perfect peace whose mind is stayed on you, because he trusts in you." I'd been in a tug-of-war with bitter thoughts and feelings. I'd get over it for a while and enjoy a bitter-free life, then an instance or memory would bring it right back.

I questioned if I'd really ever gotten past the hurt. From my point of view, I had been wronged, accused, and treated unfairly. My perceived mistreatment flooded my thoughts until I was drowning in it. I needed answers. God is and has always been my

Healer and Deliverer. How could I let bitterness come at me with a vengeance, threatening to destroy all the progress I'd made toward healing?

It was time to declare war on bitterness. I could not let it steal the blessings God had planned for me and my family. I knew I had to fight, so I prayed, lamented, and wrestled one night until the arrival of the sun the next morning. After a fitful night of limited sleep, something amazing happened the following day.

God did a great work in me, and also in those I'd harbored so much bitterness toward in the past. I can't seem to adequately translate what happened into words, not without revealing more about those whose testimonies are theirs to share, not mine. All I can say with certainty is this: I didn't know it at the time, but God's plan for rescue had begun long before I uttered those same condemning words that came from Naomi, "Call me bitter." My gracious Lord poured out his peace, forgiveness, and hope in places I never thought I'd see them. Where I was once drowning in bitterness, I now felt rescued by his grace and goodness. Only our Creator God could orchestrate such a thing.

Friend, I believe God has his hand reaching out to you in your situation, too. The packed and parched land bitterness has created inside you longs for relief. God is ready and willing to soak us in his grace, providing the relief we long for, but we also must be willing to guard against bitterness and keep it from coming in. Otherwise, God's attempts to saturate us in his grace will prove futile.

A SPIRIT OF GRACE

I've heard all the advice about how we're only hurting ourselves by harboring bitterness in our hearts, and the only way to find peace is to "give it to God." I thought I'd developed a clear understanding of the danger bitterness brings into my life. Then one unexpected incident of being cast aside and mistreated tipped the scale in bitterness' favor.

The enemy wants us to feel detached from the joy, contentment, and blessings that come from our identity as children of God. Living in this separated place can pull us away from the person God created us to be. Instead of letting bitterness change us into someone we don't recognize, we can choose God's promise of measureless grace. This interpretation of the Scripture says it well, "So here's what I've learned through it all: Leave all your cares and anxieties at the feet of the Lord, and measureless grace will strengthen you" (Psalms 55:22 TPT).

If today you're thinking like Naomi that God dealt bitterly with you and that you'll never be the same again, choose God's measureless grace as you trust the Holy Spirit to do a renewing work in you. You are not Mara.

Bitterness may lie to our hearts about who we are, but we refute bitterness by accepting God's grace.

"Then I will pour out a spirit of grace and prayer on the family of David and on the people of Jerusalem. They will look on me whom they have pierced and mourn for him as for an only son. They will grieve bitterly for him as for a firstborn son who has died" (Zechariah 12:10 NLT).

In this Scripture, the prophet Zechariah foretold the most significant event in the future of God's people—the day Jesus would give his life as a willing sacrifice for us. Historians date this prophecy roughly five hundred years before that day.[2]

Reading God's message in this passage, I think of Naomi as she made her way toward home and the excitement awaiting her there. Only, she didn't share in their enthusiasm. Let's look again at what she told everyone: "I went away full, and the Lord has brought me back empty" (Ruth 1:21a).

The King James Version translates the Hebrew word for *empty* in this verse as, "empty, without cause, void, vain." As we've walked with Naomi in her pain, we've witnessed every new void and stood with her as those voids grew together to form a canyon of heartache where bitterness, regret, and disappointment thrived. Yet even when canyons form, God offers us the one thing that will keep us from going under, "I will pour out a spirit of grace…" (Zechariah 12:10 NLT).

How could God be so generous with this gift of grace when his only Son died for my sins? I didn't deserve such mercy. So why would he do it? Why would he pour out a spirit of grace, just for me?

Because God promised never to leave us helpless and alone.

God already saw the tears we would cry as he lifted an unbearable burden from us and placed it on the cross through his Son, Jesus. God knew we would need grace. He knew we would feel empty, just like Naomi. The grace God poured out to the Israelites after years of emptiness continues to flow into our canyons today. It fills us over and over.

When I speak harsh words to my kids—*grace*.

When someone I love dies—*grace*.

When I'm buried under a pile of dirty dishes and laundry—*grace*.

When I make a bad choice—*grace*.

When I doubt my worth—*grace*.

When bitterness takes control—*grace*.

This means we can come to him empty today, ready to be filled. Let's remember to always thank him for paying our debts so willingly. Let's lift our hands toward God with gratitude, ready to accept his rescue by also accepting his gift of unending grace.[3]

SCAR TISSUE

A few months ago, I experienced a severe case of a condition known as frozen shoulder. One day I accidentally touched a hot burner on the stove, and my reflexes took over. I jerked my arm back with so much force, I tore something in my shoulder.

Then a crazy thing happened. Each day I noticed less and less range of motion until I could no longer raise my arm at all. My orthopedic doctor explained that my body had built up scar tissue around the wounded shoulder over and over again, to keep me from moving it and possibly injuring it further—an amazing example of our human body's intricate design.

Scar tissue is a defense mechanism our body uses to protect wounds and guard against further damage. Over time too much scar tissue can lock down the old wound and prevent healing.

For healing to happen, the scar tissue must be broken down a little at a time. The only way to do that is to create something called "micro-tears" under the care of a qualified physical therapist. It's a painful process, but without it, healing may not happen.

Our hearts can be a lot like that frozen shoulder when it comes to healing from bitterness.

When we experience deep hurt, our instinct is to put up a wall around our hearts to prevent further hurt. We want to live in freedom from bitterness, but those walls are tough, fortified with months or even years of protective layers. So, how do we invite healing to happen in our hearts, where the scar tissue of bitterness has built up over time?

Naomi described herself as "bitter." And honestly, I'd say she had every right to feel that way. She lost not only her husband but her two children as well. Her whole world. No doubt layers of scar tissue had built around Naomi's fragile heart. We find evidence of this as we take a step back just a few verses to a conversation Naomi had with Ruth and Orpah. From their interaction, we see Naomi already in the grip of bitterness, well before she arrived back home in Bethlehem.

Naomi urged her daughters-in-law to return home rather than accompany her to Bethlehem. Naomi said, "... No, my daughters, *my life is much too bitter* for you to share, because the Lord's hand has turned against me" (Ruth 1:12–13 CSB, Emphasis mine).

We have no way of knowing exactly when Naomi's battle with bitterness began; we do know she didn't want the bitterness she felt to spill over to her daughters-in-law.

CHAPTER 6 — BITTER WOMAN

In my own personal experience, grief can often trigger bitterness. Despair can lead to questions, like, "How could God let such a horrible thing happen?"

We may feel God has abandoned us or doesn't care about our grief. Left unchecked, bitterness can develop, pushing us away from our Holy God who loves us and wants to comfort us in our deepest sorrow.

Healing can be painful. I learned that firsthand in my visits to the physical therapist as he pushed and pulled my shoulder, one grueling millimeter at a time. I had to pray through each agonizing movement and allow it to bring me one step closer to freedom and motion. We can do the same with our bitter places, saying "yes" to whatever it takes to find healing, while knowing there may be pain in the process. Bitterness may have grown, but time gives room for healing to take place if we choose to turn to God's promises in the pain.

THE BLAME GAME

The lies formed by bitterness can lead us to believe we've been mistreated by God.

The world would have us point a finger at other people for what we've endured and to believe there's always someone else to blame. As daughters of the King, we may be tempted to turn that blame toward the God who loves us and cares for us as his children. Naomi showed us what that layer of blame looked like. In her announcement of her altered identity, Naomi played the blame game with God, saying, "...the Lord has caused me to suffer and the Almighty has sent such tragedy upon me" (Ruth 1:21 NLT). She wanted someone else to carry the responsibility, so she pointed a finger toward God.

I'm not judging Naomi for what she said that day. I've been there, accusing God for not answering my prayer the way I wanted. I've been angry with God before, and I dare to assume I'm not alone. Thankfully, God lavishes us with lovingkindness and invites us to come to him with our resentment. And when we do come to him, we need to stay there. We need to linger, not turn away or shut him out. May we choose to approach God, ready to remain in his presence as long as it takes for bitterness to uproot. May we come to him with humility, believing God will provide the help we seek. God is *for* us—a truth that will replace the root of bitterness and cause beauty to come forth.

When I recognize the root of bitterness beginning to form, I call upon this powerful Scripture to remind myself that God is just. He cannot act unjustly toward us; it isn't in his character.

"He is the Rock, his works are perfect, and all his ways are just. A faithful God who does no wrong, upright and just is he" (Deuteronomy 32:4 NIV).

Searching out a verse that reveals God's character helps us apply his Word directly to our situation. Feel free to use this verse the next time bitterness whispers lies to you, or do a quick Scripture search for one of your own. The Bible is full of God's attributes we can use in our battle against bitterness. They are powerful and effective.

Because of God, my attitude is shifting from that of a bitter woman to a blessed woman.

The enemy of your soul would love to see bitterness win because that means you'd forfeit the chance to see all God can do. When bitterness threatens to take us under, let's refuse to stop fighting. Hebrews 12:15 can be our call to action, "See to it that no one fails to obtain the grace of God; that no 'root of bitterness' springs up and causes trouble, and by it many become defiled."

FILLED WITH A MEASURE OF GOD'S GRACE

"So Naomi returned, and Ruth the Moabite her daughter-in-law with her, who returned from the country of Moab. And they came to Bethlehem at the beginning of barley harvest" (Ruth 1:22).

I wonder if Naomi experienced any fitful nights, wrestling with bitterness, fighting to hold on to the hope of God's promise of restoration for her and her family...asking him if he would come through as he'd done in the past. It's hard to rediscover hope when we feel like all is lost and the hurt hangs on. Yet, we know without a doubt, Naomi hadn't given up hope that God would fill her, because she returned to the place where he'd already answered a long-awaited prayer by replenishing the once dry and thirsty land.

The beginning of barley harvest signaled a season of blessing for God's people. Barley harvest came before wheat harvest in early spring.[4] Naomi's return coincided with the coming spring and a bountiful harvest. For this chapter's *measure to remember*, I'd like for us to hold on to this valuable truth. I feel a shift coming; I pray you do, too. Because of God, my attitude is shifting from that of a bitter woman to a blessed woman.

Just like Naomi's heart, the land of Bethlehem had been empty because of famine, but the Lord began to fill it once again. She would soon experience a shift, as well. Would she be willing to trade "Mara" for her true identity as a child of God? Was she ready to receive God's grace? God was about to do a transforming work in Naomi, and if we will return to him with our hearts set on his grace, he will do the same for us. Let the celebration for the upcoming harvest begin.

OUR HEART-FULL PRAYER

Thinking back on Naomi's time of famine may cause us to recall desolate times in our own lives. Let's refuse to let bitterness dig any deeper, and instead, take our hurt to the Lord. He is ready and eager to provide an outpouring of grace.

Dear God,

Thank you for your grace. I come to you in humble adoration today, seeking your forgiveness for the bitter root in my heart. Forgive me, Lord, for blaming you. Forgive me for harboring bitterness instead of seeking you in prayer. You are faithful and just. Forgive me for giving bitterness a place in my heart. I am pulling it out by the roots today and offering my dry and parched places to you. I am ready to be filled with your grace. Replenish my spirit, oh God. Help me start over with a renewed attitude. I am blessed by your goodness. Thank you for transforming me from a bitter woman to a blessed woman. In Jesus' name I pray, Amen.

REFILLED

CHAPTER 7

So, Help Me, God

"and I have filled him with the Spirit of God, with ability and intelligence, with knowledge and all craftsmanship"

EXODUS 31:3

Workers in the fields. Women preparing loaves of bread for a feast. Signs of new life abounded as Naomi and Ruth entered the once barren town. The residents of Bethlehem-Judah held on to God's promise to provide, and he responded in vibrant glory. The time to rejoice and enjoy the bounty had come, and no one was to be left out of the celebration.[1]

Everyone joined in the fun of the festivals. God made sure of that. Even the neediest of his children would not go hungry. Through his law God made a way to ensure plenty for those in need. For one, he made a way through the tithe, where the first fruits of God's abundant blessings would be given and stored for sharing. "And the Levite, because he has no portion or inheritance with you, and the sojourner, the fatherless, and the widow, who are within your towns, shall come and eat and be filled, that the Lord your God may bless you in all the work of your hands that you do" (Deuteronomy 14:29).[2]

God wanted his people to be filled. Content. Satisfied. More evidence to support the truth we see again and again through his Holy Word: God chose to be their portion.

Next, the law provided for certain people through the act of gleaning, which is where we meet up with Naomi and Ruth in the midst of conversation.

"And Ruth the Moabite said to Naomi, 'Let me go to the field and glean among the ears of grain after him in whose sight I shall find favor.' And she (Naomi) said to her, 'Go, my daughter'" (Ruth 2:2).

Every suffering person under God's law had the right to glean in the fields. Naomi knew this, but that didn't make her decision to allow Ruth to glean any easier. Gleaning was risky business, especially for a young single woman. Ruth's offer to glean on their behalf showed loyalty to Naomi, but more importantly, it showed courage in a desperate time and a willingness to trust God's providence.

Maybe Naomi took a lesson or two from her daughter-in-law Ruth, who refused to give up. Maybe a time of enjoying their traditional festivals brought Naomi renewed hope and allowed for healing to begin in her scarred heart. One thing we know for sure. With everything they'd been through and the emptiness that ensued, this was the beginning of a harvest.[3] And the beginning of harvest meant a change in the atmosphere. God had put the necessary pieces in place.

"So she set out and went and gleaned in the field after the reapers, and she happened to come to the part of the field belonging to Boaz, who was of the clan of Elimelech" (Ruth 2:3).

HELP IS ON THE WAY

In chapter two of the Book of Ruth, the scene shifts. Until now, we've viewed things solely from Naomi's perspective. We've identified with her, empathized with her, and learned from her. Now for the first time in their story, Naomi and Ruth separated. Naomi stayed home while Ruth ventured out on her own, determined to find a place to glean barley so she and her mother-in-law could eat.

So let's alter our course a bit and follow Ruth into the fields. We should never neglect an opportunity to join one of God's girls and witness what the Father is doing (or about to do) in her life.

"And behold, Boaz came from Bethlehem. And he said to the reapers, 'The Lord be with you!' And they answered, 'The Lord bless you.' Then Boaz said to his young man who was in charge of the reapers, 'Whose young woman is this?' And the servant who was in charge of the reapers answered, 'She is the young Moabite woman, who came back with Naomi from the country of Moab. She said, "Please let me glean and gather among the sheaves after the reapers." So she came, and she has continued from early morning until now, except for a short rest'" (Ruth 2:4–7).

The two widows needed help, so Ruth took a step of faith. When I'm in need, asking for help is a challenge. Friends, relatives, and neighbors send well-meaning texts that read, "Let me know if there's anything I can do." And I send back, "I will, thanks."

But I never do.

The truth is I'd rather not let someone get that close to my sorrow and see my frailty in all the real, ugly mess that composes my life at the time. I also forget the many examples in Scripture, and in our lives today, where God prompts others to reach out.

He uses his people to help meet the need—to fill the void.

My friend Lisa Appelo talks a lot about the beauty of receiving help from others in her book, *Life Can Be Good Again*. After her husband died, one of Lisa's friends encouraged her to make a list of tasks others could do to help—ways they could serve her and her kids. Lisa says, "Learning to ask for help means letting go of the façade that we've got it all together. It means cleaning out the plaque of pride gunking up our hearts and keeping us from admitting we need help. It means inviting others into our lack and watching God use them to meet our need."[4] Lisa reminds me to be a "gracious receiver"—something I'm still learning. I often turn to Lisa's book in my own emptiness, as it confirms I'm not alone. I can learn to open my eyes to God's miraculous ways and accept the help he sends through others when I'm tempted to linger too long in my solitude. "My help comes from the Lord, who made heaven and earth" (Psalm 121:2).

Ruth was about to receive help, too, in the form of an honorable man named Boaz. Ruth showed humble obedience to a God she was just getting to know, but she would have to let down any guard of self-sufficiency in order to allow this unexpected helper to do what only he could do. The Bible tells us Ruth "happened to" come to Boaz's field, but we know all too well, there are no coincidences when God guides the way. God's plan included Ruth and Boaz's connection all along.

Boaz noticed Ruth right away; his attitude and actions toward his new acquaintance showed his trustworthy nature. Boaz instructed Ruth to stay in his field where she'd be safe. In addition to that, he gave her access to vessels of water to satisfy her thirst.

"Then Boaz said to Ruth, 'Now, listen, my daughter, do not go to glean in another field or leave this one, but keep close to my young women. Let your eyes be on the field that they are reaping, and go after them. Have I not charged the young men not to touch you? And when you are thirsty, go to the vessels and drink what the young men have drawn'" (Ruth 2:8–9).

Seeing the intricate details of Ruth and Boaz's first encounter makes me wonder. What might've transpired if Ruth had shunned Boaz's help? How would the story unfold for Ruth and Naomi, had Ruth relied on her own ability to provide and failed to trust God to direct her steps? God had great things in store for two women who'd experienced deep loss, hunger, and need. As Ruth listened to every word Boaz spoke, she chose to believe his generosity was an act of favor from the God who loved and cared for her.

"Then she fell on her face, bowing to the ground, and said to him, 'Why have I found favor in your eyes, that you should take notice of me, since I am a foreigner?' But Boaz answered her, 'All that you have done for your mother-in-law since the death of your husband has been fully told to me, and how you left your father and mother and your native land and came to a people that you did not know before'" (Ruth 10–11).

Boaz called upon God to fill Ruth's empty places in ways beyond what she could ever hope. He asked for a "full reward" from the God of Israel, the only One who knows the intricate details of our emptiness and what will ultimately satisfy.

Like Ruth and Naomi, God stands ready to send help in our deepest, darkest times. Our cries for help haven't gone into an abyss where they will fade into faint sounds of hopelessness. No, my friend. God hears every one of them. And just as he sent help to Ruth through Boaz, he will send help to you and reassure you that your full reward waits at the end of your struggle. We can read this blessing from Boaz as a word from the Lord to us today: "The Lord repay you for what you have done, and a full reward be given you by the Lord, the God of Israel, under whose wings you have come to take refuge!" (Ruth 2:12).

A HELPER WHO'S ALWAYS AVAILABLE

"The earth was without form and void, and darkness was over the face of the deep. And the Spirit of God was hovering over the face of the waters" (Genesis 1:2).

I've heard it said that when we say goodbye to someone, part of our heart goes with them. A husband leaves, and no explanation will justify the hurt. We struggle as we watch our grown children traverse adulthood. An aging parent or spouse is here with us physically, but the person we once knew isn't *here*. We juggle the myriad emotions and responsibilities involved with caring for them. A void left behind by a loved one's absence, in whatever way, may mean we need to fill in gaps. Take on extra responsibilities. Give of our time and energy when we don't have much left to give. Our minds may even entertain thoughts like, "I didn't sign up for this." Mounting responsibilities can compound in our empty spaces. Even though we want to handle those responsibilities with grace and trust in God, we know we need help.

I've had email conversations with women just like us who've cried out to God in the void, yet still suffer—brave women who know God is real and that he cares, but can't see him at work in their circumstances. Who ask for help but hear only silence. I keep those emails tucked away safely in my online folder, so I can pray for us all. Within the void, we often need a reminder of this powerful truth from a most Holy God. Sometimes God sends help through his people. Other times he sends his Holy Spirit.

Honestly, I wish I could be more confident in the Holy Spirit working in and through me. Many times I feel like I'm standing on the earth as the Bible describes it in Genesis 1:2, formless and void, and the Holy Spirit is hovering overhead but never coming down to meet me. I stand, staring at the sky with longing, but hearing nothing. In those times, I will hang back instead of taking a step with confidence because I'm unsure of the right move. I ask for the Holy Spirit to guide me, but freeze in the uncertainty of my own ability to hear him clearly.

Friend, I hope you can read the intensity in my voice as I speak this often misunderstood truth to both of us. We need to hear it again right now. The Holy Spirit is here. For every believer in Jesus, saved by the shedding of his blood on the cross, God's Spirit is available to help us every day, every hour, every minute. Isn't that amazing news? Let's first take a look at the Holy Spirit's role in the Old Testament, back in Naomi's day, and find out more about how this powerful force from heaven came to camp out with you and me today.

"The Old Testament has a rich record of the work of the Spirit, but He was not poured out on all flesh."[5] In other words, God's precious Spirit has been around since the beginning of time. The Spirit of God did not dwell among his people back then, but he did empower certain people for certain tasks. One of these men was named Bezalel.

"The Lord said to Moses, 'See, I have called by name Bezalel the son of Uri, son of Hur, of the tribe of Judah, and I have filled him with the Spirit of God, with ability and intelligence, with knowledge and all craftsmanship'" (Exodus 31:1–3).

God gave Moses super-specific details about the furnishings for the tabernacle and courtyard in the book of Exodus. He equipped men with the skills needed to do the work, but God mentioned Bezalel by name as a man he filled with the Spirit. God gifted Bezalel with what he needed to attend to the job assigned to him, including craft skills, knowledge, and ability.

At another time in Israel's rich history, the Spirit of God came upon a man named Gideon. This son of Joash didn't appear strong and faithful where the angel of the Lord met him, sifting wheat in a winepress so the oppressive Midianites wouldn't find it. Yet the angel said, "The Lord is with you, mighty warrior"

(Judges 6:12 NIV). God asked the unassuming Gideon to do hard things. God also sent his Spirit to help. "Then the Spirit of the Lord came on Gideon, and he blew a trumpet, summoning the Abiezrites to follow him. He (Gideon) sent messengers throughout Manasseh, calling them to arms" (Judges 6:34–35a NIV).

God's Spirit gave Samson strength to stand against the Philistines,[6] Saul the boldness to become king,[7] and Joshua courage to lead the Israelites into the Promised Land.[8] Each time God's Spirit empowered his people by meeting their needs for the task ahead and for his ultimate glory.[9] I'd say God's acts of filling these men with the Spirit was a pretty special thing, indeed.

He chose them.

He called them.

He appointed them.

He equipped them.

He *helped* them.

The stories of these men inspire my spirit, and if that were the end, I'd be okay with it. But it isn't the end. Because God made it possible for us to be counted among these men filled with the Spirit of God.

Jesus himself, the sinless Son of God, said, "And I will ask the Father, and he will give you another Helper, to be with you forever, even the Spirit of truth, whom the world cannot receive, because it neither sees him nor knows him. You know him, for he dwells with you and will be in you" (John 14:16–17).

When Jesus ascended to heaven to be with the Father, the Spirit of God descended. We have within us, God's Spirit, who will give us exactly what we need for the responsibilities set before us. The same Spirit that gave courage to Joshua, faith to Gideon, strength to Samson, and wisdom to Bezalel, is here and ready to step into our emptiness and handle any situation with great precision and power. Let me be the first to remind you the Lord is with you, mighty warrior.

A SATISFIED HEART

"And at mealtime Boaz said to her, 'Come here and eat some bread and dip your morsel in the wine.' So she sat beside the reapers, and he passed to her roasted grain. And she ate until she was *satisfied*, and she had some left over" (Ruth 2:14, Emphasis mine).

As we began this chapter, we discovered how God planned everything out to provide for his people. We saw the beginnings of God's great design to help in Deuteronomy 14:29, "...the sojourner, the fatherless, and the widow, who are within your towns, shall come and eat and be filled." Now, as we close our time on Ruth and Boaz's first interaction, we see that truth in full color through the lives of these two faithful servants of God.

The Hebrew word *saba* used in Deuteronomy 14:29 to describe God's people as "filled" is the very same word describing Ruth as "satisfied."[10]

"The eyes of all look to you, and you give them their food in due season. You open your hand; you satisfy the desire of every living thing" (Psalm 145:15–16).

Through the helpful hand of Boaz, Ruth ate until satisfied—a foreshadowing of things to come for both Ruth and Naomi. But Boaz's generosity did not end there. He provided even

God fills us with his Spirit. He is our Always Available Helper.

more than an amount that would satisfy her for the moment. He helped way beyond her present hope. He provided for her need in measures that would usher in hope for a content future.

"When she rose to glean, Boaz instructed his young men, saying, 'Let her glean even among the sheaves, and do not reproach her. And also pull out some from the bundles for her and leave it for her to glean, and do not rebuke her.' So she gleaned in the field until evening. Then she beat out what she had gleaned, and it was about an ephah of barley" (Ruth 2:15–17).

FILLED WITH THE SPIRIT OF GOD

The sun descended on the field where Ruth gleaned that day. God met her in her need, just as he does when we cry out, "Please help, God!" Our Holy Helper hears our request and meets us right where we are, every time. Let's bring this chapter to a close with this *measure to remember*.

God fills us with his Spirit. He is our Always Available Helper.

"And she took it up and went into the city. Her mother-in-law saw what she had gleaned. She also brought out and gave her what food she had left over after being satisfied" (Ruth 2:18).

Ruth revealed her bounty from a hard but satisfying day's work. Her eyes may have been filled with uncertainty as she left their home that morning, but now her eyes shone like the setting sun, full of promise. She recounted every detail of her eventful day to her mother-in-law, Noami.

"And her mother-in-law said to her, 'Where did you glean today? And where have you worked? Blessed be the man who took notice of you.' So she told her mother-in-law with whom she had worked and said, 'The man's name with whom I worked today is Boaz.' And Naomi said to her daughter-in-law, 'May he be blessed by the Lord, whose kindness has not forsaken the living or the dead!' Naomi also said to her, 'The man is a close relative of ours, one of our redeemers'" (Ruth 2:19–20).

OUR HEART-FULL PRAYER

In today's chapter of Ruth and Naomi's life, we witnessed how God put the necessary puzzle pieces in place so these two determined women would get help at the right time. And only God could provide this kind of help. Ruth's first encounter with Boaz provided a picture of what happens when we cry out to God for help. Sometimes he sends help through a person; other times by filling us with his Spirit. Naomi brought the second chapter of Ruth to a close with an exclamation of Boaz's goodness. Was Naomi coming around to seeing God's divine providence? Was she positioning her emptiness to receive whatever God had for her? I believe the answers will unfold as we move forward. First, let's turn the page on this chapter with a heart-full prayer for God to send his Holy Spirit. I could use a fresh filling right now. How about you?

Dear God,

Thank you for the way you send help at just the right time. Sometimes I call out to you, "Help me, God," but I don't feel like you are near. Father, I know you are with me. Your Word declares it. Jesus came into my heart and became my Savior.

When he went to be with you, you graciously sent your Holy Spirit to guide, help, and comfort me. Thank you for your Holy Spirit's work in my life. Thank you for showing me how to be confident in the Spirit's guidance. He is with me right now. Fill me with your Spirit and let his presence in my life be evident to everyone around me. In Jesus' name I pray, Amen.

REFILLED

CHAPTER 8

Even More

"Return to the Lord your God, for he is gracious and merciful, slow to anger, and abounding in steadfast love..."

JOEL 2:13B

Until now, Naomi had little to look forward to. Hearing about Boaz, however, renewed her hope.

Boaz. A kinsman redeemer who could provide for her and Ruth, and possibly carry on the family name. Could this be a turnaround in her otherwise dire circumstances? Was the God of Abraham, Isaac, and Jacob hearing her cries after all?

It had been a hard road, no doubt about it. But she couldn't argue with the fact that no matter how much she'd lost, she served a God of restoration. Naomi needed only to look out her front door for confirmation. God replenished the once barren land of her people. Just look at what Ruth brought back from the fields after gleaning for one day! So, since God did this amazing thing for his land and his people, then maybe...

God had even more restoration in store.

"And Naomi said to Ruth, her daughter-in-law, 'It is good, my daughter, that you go out with his young women, lest in another field you be assaulted.' So she kept close to the young women of Boaz, gleaning until the end of the barley and wheat harvests. And she lived with her mother-in-law" (Ruth 2:22–23).

MASTER RESTORER

The noise of home remodeling threatens to disrupt my thoughts at this very moment. I've been trying to get those thoughts on paper every day this week, with no success. This morning, I stand before my laptop once again, notes spread out in a half-circle around me, hoping I can make progress. Unfortunately, people in and out of the front door, an electric saw, and lots of hammering are winning the battle for my concentration.

I feel like I've been here before. Three years ago, we had our aging bathroom updated with the latest features including new floors, countertops, sinks, tub, and shower—a pricey renovation, but something we'd wanted for a long time. Imagine my disappointment when a couple of weeks ago, I noticed water stains creeping up the wall closest to the shower. A clear problem had formed behind the lovely exterior of our bathroom renovation.

It pained me to see the beautiful gray tile and coordinating river rock demolished by a master contractor, so he could get to the root of the issue. All that work. All that money. All the time and effort, literally down the drain. Over time, the problem would have caused extensive damage. It's a good thing we noticed something amiss and called in the master shower installer to redo the job.

My expectations for God's restoring work in my life can be a lot like my expectations for a shiny new bathroom. I have my own idea what I want the restoration to look like. I hold firm to those expectations, even though God wants me to let go, so he can do something new and unexpected. I hurry past any potential pitfalls God warns me about, so I can smile and say, "It's exactly how I envisioned it!" While I set my sights on the outside, God is more concerned with the restoration that happens on the inside.

I can say with certainty I'm not alone in the search for true restoration and what that means according to God's Word. I have email after email from readers just like you and me, wanting to know if and when God will restore what was lost in their lives. A few years ago, I wrote a post on kristinebrown.net explaining what the Bible says about restoration. (A quick Google search, and the blog post will pop up for you, if you're interested.) That post continues to be the most read post on my website, month after month. And even though I learned much about God as our Master Restorer through researching for that article, I still wrestle with letting God restore in his way, in his timing, and for his purpose in my life.

We understand, like Naomi did, that we serve a God of restoration. We've seen him restore fortunes to Job, freedom to the Israelites, a future for Rahab, and a family line to Sarah and Abraham. So why do we have such difficulty letting God get behind the walls of our heart? Why can we only imagine a fulfilled life when God restores our circumstances according to our expectations?

When we ask God to restore a relationship, a job, or family, we often think the result will look similar, if not the same, as it did before the void happened. We hold the memories of our best life so dear. They become something we put on a pedestal, and anything else beyond them pales in comparison.

Friend, our lives may not look the same after loss cuts into the surface of our hearts. But if we can hand those missing pieces over to God with spirits reliant on him, our finite minds cannot conceive the wondrous things God will do. We need to be willing to let him control the how, when, and why of what needs to be restored. To do this, we commit to prayerfully seek him daily. Then we will hold less to temporary things and more to the unfathomable goodness of an All-Knowing God, who is ready to restore what was lost.

"I will restore to you the years that the swarming locust has eaten, the hopper, the destroyer, and the cutter, my great army, which I sent among you" (Joel 2:25).

THRESHING FLOOR

Naomi had lost so much. Surely she found it hard to imagine life beyond the empty spaces. Now one thing after another began lining up in her favor, so she made the choice to lean into the possibilities God showed her. She approached Ruth with renewed purpose.

"...My daughter, should I not seek rest for you, that it may be well with you? Is not Boaz our relative, with whose young women you were? See, he is winnowing barley tonight at the threshing floor. Wash therefore and anoint yourself, and put on your cloak and go down to the threshing floor, but do not make yourself known to the man until he has finished eating and drinking. But when he lies down, observe the place where he lies. Then go and uncover his feet and lie down, and he will tell you what to do'" (Ruth 3:1–4).

Naomi's instruction needs a bit of clarification for our twenty-first century minds. Our experiences with courtship differ from Naomi's day, so her advice to Ruth may seem strange. Something to keep in mind as we follow Ruth to where Boaz celebrated at the threshing floor while keeping a close eye on his harvest: the important work of separating grain from the chaff happened at the threshing floor. By spending the night there, landowners could protect their grain from thieves. That's where Ruth would find Boaz, asleep in a place usually reserved for men. But Naomi knew Boaz would understand Ruth's actions and keep her dignity intact.[1]

"And she (Ruth) replied, 'All that you say I will do.' So she went down to the threshing floor and did just as her mother-in-law had commanded her" (Ruth 3:5–6).

Let's also keep in mind that after barley harvest came wheat harvest with a time span of seven weeks between Passover and the Festival of Weeks. Since the barley crop was ready to harvest by Passover, we can infer from this timeline that by the time Ruth visited Boaz at the threshing floor, they were no longer strangers. "The couple would have actually known each other for quite some time."[2]

The threshing floor was a place where God's abundance could not only be seen and touched, but experienced to the full. Surrounded by bounty, men rejoiced over mounds of blessings provided by a God who promised to restore beyond the destruction. Even the prophet Joel spoke of the importance of the threshing floor in his word from the Lord:

> "Be glad, O children of Zion,
>
> and rejoice in the Lord your God,
> for he has given the early rain for your vindication;
> he has poured down for you abundant rain,
> the early and the latter rain, as before.
>
> The threshing floors shall be full of grain;
> the vats shall overflow with wine and oil.
> I will restore to you the years
> that the swarming locust has eaten,
> the hopper, the destroyer, and the cutter,
> my great army, which I sent among you.
>
> You shall eat in plenty and be satisfied,
> and praise the name of the Lord your God,
> who has dealt wondrously with you
>
> And my people shall never again be put to shame."
>
> JOEL 2:23–26

Just before Joel spoke this message of restoration to God's people, a swarm of locusts had destroyed the land. Joel compared the natural disaster to God's powerful army on the day of judgement. "The fields are ruined, the ground is dried up, the grain is destroyed, the new wine is dried up, the oil fails" (Joel 1:10 NIV). Joel used that event as a call to repentance, ". . . Return to the Lord your God, for he is gracious and compassionate, slow to anger and abounding in love, and he relents from sending calamity" (Joel 2:13 NIV). God sent his message through the prophet, "where there is repentance, there is hope."[3]

The three short chapters in the book of Joel bring my mind and heart back to the day Naomi and her beloved Elimelech left Bethlehem-Judah for Moab. How the land appeared desolate and their hope floundered. But over and over, God demonstrated his faithfulness to those whose hope rested in him alone, "You shall eat in plenty and be satisfied, and praise the name of the Lord your God, who has dealt wondrously with you" (Joel 2:26).

FILLED WITH GOD'S ABUNDANCE

The language of the land, like in the prophet's speech, was something farmers could relate to. A lush and fertile ground equaled God's provision, restoration, and overflowing goodness. The NLT Study Bible puts it this way, "Nature shows God's generosity—giving us more than we need or deserve."[4] Joel's message is ripe with references to God's abundance—the same abundance more than 5,000 people witnessed when a young boy took his five barley loaves and two fish to Jesus.

It's no coincidence that the bread the boy took to Jesus was made from barley. "The Passover, the feast of the Jews, was at hand," (John 6:4) and barley was considered the first fruits of the season because it matured for harvest a month before wheat, in time for the Passover meal. Barley bread was a staple for the poor, and our God is no respecter of persons.[5] His provision became a bountiful feast for everyone who heard Jesus' message that day.

"Jesus then took the loaves, and when he had given thanks, he distributed them to those who were seated. So also the fish, as much as they wanted" (John 6:11).

Enough men, women, and children to fill a stadium sat on a hillside listening to words that would change their lives forever. With empty bellies, empty hands, and equally empty hearts, they hungered and thirsted for something to nourish them beyond the here and now. And in true Jesus-style, the multiplied bread and fish not only satisfied everyone there, they also had an abundance leftover.

"And when they had eaten their fill, he told his disciples, 'Gather up the leftover fragments, that nothing may be lost.' So they gathered them up and filled twelve baskets with fragments from the five barley loaves left by those who had eaten" (John 6:12–13).

God's abundance filled the land in Joel's prophesy.

God's abundance filled 5,000 bellies with only five barley loaves and two fish.

God's abundance filled Ruth's stomach the day she met Boaz, with enough left over for Naomi.

My dear sister in Christ, if you have any doubt we serve a God of abundance, let these testimonies crush that doubt into a million pieces. Just like God's generosity flowed into the lives of his children then, he has marvelous plans to pour an overabundance into your life and mine. Let's sit with that thought for a moment. It's worth our time and attention. Because remember, we can get caught up in how we expect things to be and miss the beauty of what God is doing. And I don't know about you, but I don't want to miss a thing. So to settle the matter once and for all, let's see what the psalmist says about it.

"You crown the year with a bountiful harvest; even the hard pathways overflow with abundance" (Psalm 65:11 NLT).

There will be times in our lives when empty spaces and hard pathways seem to rule. Times when voids take up so much space, there's hardly anything left of the foundation we need to keep steady. We tend toward closing off those places to protect what little space we have, all the while fearing one more void will destroy what's left. But we know with absolute certainty that God is preparing us for a harvest. We never have to doubt that, and until such time the harvest arrives, God wants us to open our emptiness before him and trust him with it.

When we come before the Father with an open heart, it feels vulnerable, scary, even. But it's exactly the posture we need to take in order to show him we are ready to rely on him at all times: the abundant times, the scarce times, and everything in between.

OPEN HANDS, OPEN HEART

Ruth didn't know what to expect when she approached her potential redeemer with an open heart. But she trusted the wisdom of her mother-in-law and God's guiding hand. Boaz didn't recognize Ruth at first, shocked to see someone there in the middle of the night. "Around midnight Boaz suddenly woke up and turned over. He was surprised to find a woman lying at his feet! 'Who are you?' he asked. 'I am your servant Ruth,' she replied. 'Spread the corner of your covering over me, for you are my family redeemer'" (Ruth 3:8–9 NLT).

The word "corner" literally translates to "wings," letting Boaz know of his role to serve as God's protective wing over Ruth.[6] Once Boaz noticed Ruth's presence, he greeted her by acknowledging her overflowing loyalty to Naomi.

"'The Lord bless you, my daughter!' Boaz exclaimed. 'You are showing *even more* family loyalty now than you did before, for you have not gone after a younger man, whether rich or poor. Now don't worry about a thing, my daughter. I will do what is necessary, for everyone in town knows you are a virtuous woman'" (Ruth 3:10–11 NLT Emphasis mine).

The two needed to wait until just before dawn in order for Ruth to leave undetected. But before saying their farewells, Boaz made the single most significant gesture when it comes to God's plan for our emptiness—a gesture that encompassed the lesson Naomi would soon learn, and one I believe God wants us to discover through the pages of this book.

Boaz filled Ruth's garment with six measures of barley to deliver to Naomi, because he did not want Ruth to go back to Naomi empty-handed.

"And he said, 'Bring the garment you are wearing and hold it out.' So she held it, and he measured out six measures of bar-

Boaz's gift of grain for Naomi represented God abundantly filling the emptiness Naomi once felt.

ley and put it on her. Then she went into the city. And when she came to her mother-in-law, she said, 'How did you fare, my daughter?' Then she told her all that the man had done for her, saying, "These six measures of barley he gave to me, for he said to me, 'You must not go back empty-handed to your mother-in-law'" (Ruth 3:15–17).

Our *measure to remember* is this: Boaz's gift of grain for Naomi represented God abundantly filling the emptiness Naomi once felt.

How can we know this? How can we be certain God planned to pour out an abundance into Naomi's heart? Because the word *rêqām*, meaning "empty-handed," is the same Hebrew word Naomi spoke in Ruth 1:21 at the beginning of our journey together: "I went away full, and the Lord has brought me back empty."

The process of refilling had begun. Just as Ruth approached the threshing floor with open hands and an open heart, Naomi needed to be open to God's restoring work. That's not an easy thing to do when you've felt the sting of one void after another for so long. But Naomi had taken baby steps toward healing and renewing her hope in God. God was changing the way Naomi viewed her emptiness, and he is doing the same for you and me.

FULL HANDS, FULL HEART

Before Naomi left Bethlehem-Judah, there were scorched lands, empty bellies, and funerals. Since her return, there had been harvesting, feasting, and celebrating. Naomi trusted Boaz to do what he said. Another demonstration of hope's renewal.

"She replied, 'Wait, my daughter, until you learn how the matter turns out, for the man will not rest but will settle the matter today'" (Ruth 3:18).

Naomi trusted Boaz to do what he said he would do. She trusted God to restore what the locusts had eaten. Here, we find her quite the distance from the place we started with this precious woman of faith. Yet we have even more to discover on our visit, because God has even more in store.

OUR HEART-FULL PRAYER

God's abundance runs through Naomi's story like an ever-flowing spring filling a dried-up riverbed. Let's rely on him to fill us to overflowing from his generous supply. Let's open our hands and hearts to the Father, even if we feel vulnerable or scared. Restoration awaits as we take on a posture of complete trust.

Dear God,

Thank you for your abundance in my life. Your Word says, "You crown the year with a bountiful harvest; even the hard pathways overflow with abundance" (Psalm 65:11 NLT). You are a generous God, and I know you have good plans to restore the empty spaces in my heart. Forgive me for expecting you to restore according to my will instead of yours. You are sovereign, and your ways are best. Help me to release my expectations and see the beauty of what you are doing in my life. The void I have over past hurt has left a dry, hardened place. Yet your goodness flows freely and provides even more than I could ask for. My hope is renewed. Thank you for filling me to overflowing. In Jesus' name, Amen.

REFILLED

CHAPTER 9

In a New Light

"I pray that your hearts will be flooded with light so that you can understand the confident hope he has given to those he called—his holy people who are his rich and glorious inheritance"

EPHESIANS 1:18 NLT

All I could see through the screen of our newly purchased tent was pure darkness. My young son and I huddled together as I searched for sleep after a long day of outdoor activities. Hiking, horseback riding, and making crafts all took their toll. Our night under the stars would finish off this mother/son adventure, but the sweltering Texas heat with no breeze was just too much. I needed to escape our two-person unit (that was really only big enough for one). I had a little problem though. It was dark out there. Thankfully, I spotted another boy-mom making her way out of her tent.

My camping skills were lackluster at best, but you'd think I'd at least know to keep a lantern on hand for such an occasion. Unfortunately, I didn't. So I hustled over close to my fellow scouting mom and stood near her lantern. I felt like the Israelites led by the fire in the wilderness, "And the Lord went before them by day in a pillar of cloud to lead them along the way, and by night in a pillar of fire to give them light, that they might travel by day and by night" (Exodus 13:21). In the darkness of the woods, standing near the light gave me a clear view of my surroundings.

As a young child, I remember pitching a tent in my own backyard with neighborhood friends, holding our flashlights up toward the roof, making shadow animals with our hands. Those long summer nights held such sweet memories of laughter and friendship. I wanted the same for my son. I wanted to make so many memories it would take a dozen bookshelves to contain all the photo albums and scrapbooks. Those days whisk by too quickly.

Doesn't seem like that long ago, but many summers and campouts have come and gone from then until now, and so has my identity as a *boy-mom*. Catching lizards in the yard and buying supplies for science fair projects have been replaced with texting to see if he had a good day and getting together for a meal when we can. Some days I stare out the window into the backyard and think about what I would give for one more lizard chase.

CHAPTER 9 — IN A NEW LIGHT

Then God reminds me of a grander plan. The seasons of life shape who we are, and that change is as natural as the sunrise on a fall morning or the sparkle of lightening bugs on a summer night. Still, on quiet days my mind has time to wander, and the memories of how things used to be bring back my awareness of the void left behind in a momma's empty nest.

I remember the last semester of our son's senior year. I decided it was time for me to resign from my teaching job to focus on writing full time. I had taken that teaching job the year we moved to town and our son started kindergarten. He and I had driven to school together most days of the last thirteen years, and we even spent a few years on the same campus. Much of my identity centered on school life. I carried my title as "Mrs. Brown, seventh grade English teacher" with pride. So as our boy walked across the graduation stage, and I walked out of an empty classroom for the last time, I didn't expect the void to hit with such ferocity. I wanted to embrace the freedom to enjoy the adventures ahead. Instead, I mourned over losing who I was.

WHOSE I AM

At this point in the chapter, I would usually skip back to Naomi's life and find out what God wants to show us in the next page of her story. But I'm going to resist the urge to follow the usual path. This seems like the perfect place to take a seat on a nearby rock and talk for a spell about some very real and raw feelings created when *who we are* changes.

The reality of knowing you're totally replaceable can shake the foundation of even the most confident of us. You've been a part of something, then suddenly you aren't, and systems keep moving without you. Sure, people say kind things like, "You'll be missed." But a busy year begins, and you're reminded just how infinitely small you are in the big picture.

Girl, I get it. Let's just spill it all right here on this rock, you and me. I don't know what I was thinking the day I decided to resign the same season I entered an empty nest. The first few days of that newfound freedom brought sadness and regret. The truth is, I no longer felt needed. And if one more person used the word "retirement" in my presence, I was going to scream. I hated that word. *Retire.* So dismal, so permanent.

My consciousness of the voids grew. I tried to put things on the calendar to help me stay connected with people and places I associated with that season of life, so I could still feel part of something. I volunteered, met friends for lunch, stayed in touch with former students, now grown with plans of their own. But all those efforts gave temporary fulfillment. Inside the voids, I saw pure darkness. But God has a way of giving light when his children need it most.

"For it is you who light my lamp; the Lord my God lightens my darkness" (Psalm 18:28).

After a few short months, I found myself staring into yet another dark place, more intimidating than anything I'd experienced before. I share about my cancer journey in detail in another book, but for our purposes here it's important for me to mention it as a testimony to God's perfect timing. Standing on the cusp of this awful thing called cancer, God gave me clarity about the changes in my circumstances—about our empty nest, leaving my job of thirteen years, everything.

CHAPTER 9 — IN A NEW LIGHT

As I sought his wisdom and peace for our next steps, he held the lantern out. He showed me how I would need the time at home for treatments and healing. There was no way I could've kept working in the classroom while battling that type of cancer. And knowing our boy was off on an adventure beyond high school gave me the space and rest I would need that would not have been available even a year before. I could take a breath, stop staring into the darkness of the void, and know my Heavenly Father had it handled. *Who I was* paled in comparison to *whose I was.*

GUIDING LIGHT

Scripture is filled with beautiful references to light. We see God's Word described as light in Psalm 119:105, "Your word is a lamp before my feet and a light for my journey" (Common English Bible). Jesus described himself as light in John 8:12, "I am the light of the world. Whoever follows me will not walk in darkness, but will have the light of life." We will explore Jesus, the Light of Life, in chapter eleven. For this chapter, let's pull our focus verse from something Paul said in his letter to the church at Ephesus. I believe his words will resonate with those of us who've devoted much time and energy gazing at the darkness the void provides (raising my hand here). The apostle Paul prayed God would flood their hearts with light.

"I pray that your hearts will be flooded with light so that you can understand the confident hope he has given to those he called—his holy people who are his rich and glorious inheritance" (Ephesians 1:18 NLT).

The ESV puts it this way, "having the eyes of your hearts enlightened, that you may know what is the hope to which he has called you, what are the riches of his glorious inheritance in the saints." I don't know about you, friend, but the eyes of my heart don't always turn toward the light when they should. They fixate on holes and nurse the wounds of what's missing instead of seeing all the good things God willed for me to receive.

Your life and mine are filled with riches of his glorious inheritance. Not always tangible riches we can put in the bank, or the kind we notice right away, but those things we've come to learn are more valuable than silver or gold. God gave us claim to these riches for his purpose and his glory, "Furthermore, because we are united with Christ, we have received an inheritance from God, for he chose us in advance, and he makes everything work out according to his plan." (Ephesians 1:11 NLT).

It's a challenge to root ourselves in our identity as God's children when so much of who we are gets wrapped up in our circumstances or seasons. It's also normal for us to cherish those times; we recognize them as gifts from God, so naturally we will feel empty when they are gone. But even though we miss what once was, we can discover the goodness of God's gifts right where we are. This verse is my go-to for strengthening my roots in not only who I am, but also whose I am: "Do not be deceived, my beloved brothers. Every good gift and every perfect gift is from above, coming down from the Father of lights, with whom there is no variation or shadow due to change" (James 1:16–17).

This verse brings much needed reset to my focus when I spend too much time gazing into the darkness of what's missing.

CHAPTER 9 — IN A NEW LIGHT

My inheritance from the Lord is the evidence of my identity as his daughter. As I turn toward the Father of lights, he will illuminate my heart and mind to the good things of my present season and comfort me in the longing for seasons past.

INHERITANCE CLAIMED

"But you are a chosen race, a royal priesthood, a holy nation, a people for his own possession, that you may proclaim the excellencies of him who called you out of darkness into his marvelous light" (1 Peter 2:9).

After Boaz assured Ruth of his intentions toward her, Naomi and Ruth waited for him to take care of matters that day. Men held the responsibility of handling those sorts of things, and Boaz had shown himself to be a man of impeccable character. Following the law of the day, Boaz headed with purpose in to town and spotted the other potential kinsman redeemer whom he'd mentioned to Ruth. This man, a closer relative than Boaz, needed to be apprised of the opportunity to claim the land belonging to Naomi's late husband, Elimelech.

We saw early in Naomi and Ruth's long, arduous journey how bleak their future appeared. A widow had no claim to her late husband's inheritance, unless, that is, a close relative stepped up and agreed to marry the widow. That would have been a difficult choice for someone already married with his own children, which we should keep in mind as we read the exchange between Boaz and his relative at the city gate.

"Now Boaz had gone up to the gate and sat down there. And behold, the redeemer, of whom Boaz had spoken, came by. So

Boaz said, 'Turn aside, friend; sit down here.' And he turned aside and sat down. And he took ten men of the elders of the city and said, 'Sit down here.' So they sat down. Then he said to the redeemer, 'Naomi, who has come back from the country of Moab, is selling the parcel of land that belonged to our relative Elimelech'" (Ruth 4:1–3).

Hearing of the availability of Elimelech's land, this unnamed man jumped at the chance to acquire it. But then, Boaz threw a curveball in the conversation, with ten willing witnesses looking on.

"The day you buy the field from the hand of Naomi, you also acquire Ruth the Moabite, the widow of the dead, in order to perpetuate the name of the dead in his inheritance" (Ruth 4:5).

A man of business savvy knew how to approach this delicate topic. I'd like to think that fact came into play as God moved things in Boaz's favor. When the man declined, citing that he could not marry Ruth, Boaz wasted no time sealing the deal, restoring Naomi and Ruth's earthly inheritance.

"Then Boaz said to the elders and all the people, 'You are witnesses this day that I have bought from the hand of Naomi all that belonged to Elimelech and all that belonged to Chilion and to Mahlon. Also Ruth the Moabite, the widow of Mahlon, I have bought to be my wife, to perpetuate the name of the dead in his inheritance, that the name of the dead may not be cut off from among his brothers and from the gate of his native place. You are witnesses this day'" (Ruth 4:9–10).

Our life circumstances will change; our inheritance as a child of God will not.

FILLED WITH LIGHT

Naomi's circumstances had changed drastically since the day she set out for Moab. In her mind, she'd left a wealthy woman, rich in love, favor, family, and all the things that equaled a fulfilled life. She also thought she had gone back to a life of a destitute and dark existence, where the best things had been stolen. Yet even though the fate of her earthly inheritance hung in the balance, her spiritual inheritance did not. It would never change, and it will never change for you and me.

Surely Naomi wondered what it would have been like to arrive home with her identity as Elimelech's wife still intact. How so much had shifted and the best of life seemed behind her. Now, God flooded Naomi's heart with light, reminding her of her rich and glorious inheritance as his precious daughter. Where Naomi once longed for what was, she now recognized her present gifts. Let's rejoice over our own present gifts with this *measure to remember*. Our life circumstances will change; our inheritance as a child of God will not.

May we rest in the knowledge of our identity *and* inheritance. We are called out of darkness into God's perfect light.

"If you are filled with light, with no dark corners, then your whole life will be radiant, as though a floodlight were filling you with light" (Luke 11:36 NLT).

OUR HEART-FULL PRAYER

Nothing can illuminate our hearts and lift our spirits like God's light. When darkness surrounds us, God calls our attention to

CHAPTER 9 — IN A NEW LIGHT

our identity and inheritance by filling us with that light. As we pray, let's allow God to flood our empty places with the light of his presence.

Dear God,

Sometimes I look straight into the darkness and let it have all of my focus. I fail to see your light that you so generously hold out for me. Forgive me for not seeing the many blessings in my life. Thank you for illuminating my heart so I can understand my inheritance as your precious child. Help me to keep my focus on you in dark circumstances. Help me know that even when all that is good in my life seems to be stolen, my spiritual inheritance can never be taken from me. Every good and perfect gift is from you, and my blessings are too numerous to count. In Jesus' name I pray, Amen.

REFILLED

CHAPTER 10

Down in My Heart, Where?

*"The Lord is my strength and shield.
I trust him with all my heart. He helps me,
and my heart is filled with joy.
I burst out in songs of thanksgiving"*

PSALM 28:7 NLT

Boaz didn't let a day pass before handling matters. That's what I call taking care of business.

When it comes to important tasks, and even not so important ones, I tend to waver back and forth, avoiding commitment for fear of making the wrong decision. But not our man of the hour. Naomi and Ruth didn't wait long for an answer because this guy made decisions with purpose. Boaz wasted no time declaring his commitment to Ruth, and the onlookers wasted no time declaring blessings over their lives, their home, and their future together.

"Then all the people who were at the gate and the elders said, 'We are witnesses. May the Lord make the woman, who is coming into your house, like Rachel and Leah, who together built up the house of Israel. May you act worthily in Ephrathah and be renowned in Bethlehem, and may your house be like the house of Perez, whom Tamar bore to Judah, because of the offspring that the Lord will give you by this young woman'" (Ruth 4:11–12).

Both Boaz and Ruth received a blessing. Ruth, the Moabite woman from the other side of the sea...a woman whose people had been enemies of the Israelites for years, but who'd shown herself loyal to her aging mother-in-law, Naomi. The leaders of the day prayed a blessing of abundance over her, mentioning the names Rachel and Leah, the wives of Jacob, whose children became the foundation of the twelve tribes of Israel.

And Boaz, the man who showed up to greet his workers in his fields at the precise moment God led Ruth there, received a blessing, too. This understated, yet wildly respected man, made the perfect match for the role of husband to Ruth. The townspeople compared his home to that of Perez who founded the leading clan of Judah, to which Boaz belonged. That blessing mentioned Tamar, whose story was a messy one, not unlike our own at times. A good reminder that, "Throughout the Bible, we see how God chooses to redeem sinners and use messy situations to bring about His purposes. He does the same today."[1]

No sooner did the blessings pour out, did these two experience the most joyful occasion of their lives. Ruth became pregnant, and they had a baby.

"So Boaz took Ruth, and she became his wife. And he went in to her, and the Lord gave her conception, and she bore a son" (Ruth 4:13).

JOY, JOY, JOY

The Israelites had cut their teeth on songs of praise. Since their exodus from slavery in Egypt, this chosen group of people crafted and sang songs of deliverance and God's mighty works. Throughout history, their songs told stories of generations before them and exuded joy in their present days. Many of the lyrics came to life in times of great distress and sorrow, still others after God performed a miracle. Thankfully we have access to many of these powerful works of art in the Book of Psalms.

I can relate to growing up with catchy church tunes of childhood days sealed in my memory. Like the Israelites, those songs serve a greater purpose in my life, even now that those childhood years stretch further and further behind me. When life takes a turn for the better, those songs come to mind as if on cue. I instantly want to celebrate what God has done. It's my way of giving thanks. I sing at the top of my lungs and I don't care who's listening, a lot like the exiles returning to Jerusalem after years in Babylon. History tells us they likely sang psalms like this one in Psalm 126:[2]

> *"When the Lord brought back his exiles to Jerusalem, it was like a dream!*
>
> *We were filled with laughter, and we sang for joy.*
>
> *And the other nations said, 'What amazing things the Lord has done for them.'*
>
> *Yes, the Lord has done amazing things for us!*
>
> *What joy!"*
>
> PSALM 126:1–3 NLT

Psalm 126 is like the ancient version of one of my all-time favorites from Sunday school, "I've got the joy, joy, joy, joy, down in my heart!" That tune could get my toes tapping and put a smile on my face better than any other. But what I love about Psalm 126 is that is doesn't stop with a shout for joy. The lyrics go on to acknowledge the pain of this life.

"Those who plant in tears will harvest with shouts of joy. They weep as they go to plant their seed, but they sing as they return with the harvest" (Psalm 126:5–6 NLT).

The psalmist relates joy to the harvest, as we've seen throughout Scripture, showing the familiar connection between bounty and rejoicing. Yet the metaphor isn't lost on us, is it? We've not only seen harvest, but we've also planted plenty of tears in the years we've sown on this earth. God doesn't expect us to ignore the hurt we feel and pretend to be joyful all the time. There are days when we won't feel joyful, and it would be wrong for me to imply otherwise.

We serve a God who cares about our hurts. He understands our tears and promises us seasons of plenty where our hearts will be filled with joy. My friend and fellow writer Doris Swift said it well, "Let's acknowledge the power of God's joy in us. His joy makes our joy full, overriding the brokenness of this world and the devastation of our circumstances. We are supernaturally filled with joy and have permission to experience it in all the seasons of our lives, not just the good ones" (Doris Swift, *Surrender the Joy Stealers*).[3]

Have you ever been deep in the throes of sorrow and lamenting before God, when out of nowhere something unexpected and beautiful catches your attention? I recall one such time, crying out to God, tears streaming, then I glanced out the window to see a vibrant red cardinal perched on the windowsill. Another time, in the midst of tear-filled prayers in my car, a favorite worship song came on the radio. Its lyrics spoke a promise straight from the Lord and reminded me how he hears my every cry and cares about every hurt. I believe those are not coincidences; they are holy moments from God to remind us of the joy he wants to give. When joy seems like an impossible dream, God shows us nothing is impossible with him.

"You have put more joy in my heart than they have when their grain and wine abound" (Psalm 4:7).

HOW TO MAKE ROOM FOR JOY

"Then the women said to Naomi, 'Blessed be the Lord, who has not left you this day without a redeemer, and may his name be renowned in Israel!'" (Ruth 4:14).

Can I share a secret? Okay, it is not so much a secret as it is something I've been holding inside but knew all along I'd get to announce eventually. Here it is. The big reveal.

I've anticipated getting to the above verse since the moment we opened to page one. The day the women surrounded Naomi demonstrated an act of solidarity, and they celebrated with her.

There's nothing quite as sweet as sisters ready to cheer for you. Some of my best days have been those spent laughing, crying, hugging, and rejoicing with women who get it. In fact, let's do that right now. Let's make a memory of our own by stepping into Naomi's circle of friends and joining the celebration. (I'm imagining tacos.) Naomi has great news to share, and she's inviting us to the party!

"Ce-le-brate good times, come on!"

Kool and the Gang sure knew how to celebrate in song with these catchy lyrics from their 1980s hit. But let's take it back a few more centuries to God's word spoken through the prophet Isaiah. This seems fitting for the occasion, "For the Lord comforts Zion; he comforts all her waste places and makes her wilderness like Eden, her desert like the garden of the Lord; joy and gladness will be found in her, thanksgiving and the voice of song" (Isaiah 51:3).

"Her" refers to Zion in this passage from the book of Isaiah, but the joy and gladness of the Lord can just as well be yours, mine, and Naomi's. The women all celebrated the birth of Naomi's grandbaby, and Naomi laid him on her lap. In her moment of great gladness, I wonder if Naomi thought about her own late sons or wished her late husband could have been there with her to enjoy the moment. I've been there, and maybe you have, too, where you're enjoying a special day or event but sensing a void of wishing someone else could be there to celebrate with you. This brings up a difficult question I don't want to pass over.

Is it possible to live with joy and live with a void at the same time?

We can be right smack in the middle of a joyful occasion when the pain of loss, betrayal, or despair returns. Sometimes the void resurfaces because we wonder what might have been.

Gratitude and praise ready
our hearts for the joy
God wants to pour in.

That void can threaten to steal the joy from whatever it is we're celebrating if we don't know how to respond, but gratitude and praise provide a solid base for joy to remain.

"The Lord is my strength and shield. I trust him with all my heart. He helps me, and my heart is filled with joy. I burst out in songs of thanksgiving" (Psalm 28:7 NLT).

Through the psalmist David's life, our creative and caring God gave us a recipe for how to blend the joy and pain that often intersect in our lives. David claimed his own heart was filled with joy, even though he was no stranger to suffering. He didn't deny the pain he felt. He acknowledged his suffering with honesty to the God he knew would listen. Then he proclaimed joy anyway.

"I pray to you, O Lord, my rock. Do not turn a deaf ear to me. For if you are silent, I might as well give up and die. Listen to my prayer for mercy as I cry out to you for help, as I lift my hands toward your holy sanctuary" (Psalm 28:1–2 NLT).

Psalm 28 shows us three things we can do to prepare our hearts for joy when emptiness returns. One: Acknowledge God hears our cries for help. Two: Accept the joy God generously pours into our hearts. Three: Praise him and give thanks. This brings us to our *measure to remember*. Gratitude and praise ready our hearts for the joy God wants to pour in.

In Scripture, gratitude and praise often accompany joy. The women surrounding Naomi demonstrated gratitude and praise in their words, "Blessed be the Lord!" So while we celebrate, let's learn a valuable spiritual lesson from our ancestors in the faith. The key to making room for joy is leaning into the gratitude and praise when everything inside us wants to back away.

CHAPTER 10 — DOWN IN MY HEART, WHERE?

TOTAL ECLIPSE

We'd heard about the upcoming eclipse for weeks. The entire country anticipated that day. I, however, tried to come up with every excuse for avoiding it, including my long list of things to do. (There's always a list.) But the morning of the much-awaited eclipse, no matter how many reasons I had for staying inside, I just kept thinking how much our girl would have loved this day. Everything about it.

She loved all things moon and planet related. She loved her telescope. She would have been totally giddy over the totality and shared lots of random space facts with us leading up to this once-in-a-lifetime experience. But we couldn't call her or share the joy that today would bring.

Usually when memories surface and I feel that familiar void in my heart over our loss, I will distract myself with other things, and there's nothing wrong with that. In fact, many times it's necessary. But on this special day I began to wonder, what would happen if we leaned into the void just a bit, even if it's scary? What might God do with the void?

So my husband and I let ourselves go there, even though everything inside screamed to back away and our hearts said the pain would be too much.

We got out around people. We made small talk with neighbors. We watched parents teaching their kids, strapping special paper sunglasses around their little heads, and pointing to the sky. We *oohed* and *aahed* and cheered at the wonder of what we had the privilege to witness. We smiled and enjoyed a hamburger hot off the grill. And do you know what God did? He filled the void with joy for the moment, and he reminded me that the void left behind in loss may not go away, but he can be the portion I need, if I will let him.

FILLED WITH THE JOY OF THE LORD

"He shall be to you a restorer of life and a nourisher of your old age, for your daughter-in-law who loves you, who is more to you than seven sons, has given birth to him" (Ruth 4:15).

Isn't it something that Naomi's friends used the phrase "restorer of life" to describe what she could expect in the years ahead because of the birth of her grandson? They also refer to him as a "nourisher" for her old age. Reminds me of what we discovered through Naomi's story in chapter four about how God provides what we need to sustain us, and in chapter eight about God as our Master Restorer. No matter how much time we spend in God's Word, I'm always amazed at how he brings his truth full circle in the lives of his people. One day we will see ours come full circle, as well.

As I pen the final words of this chapter, I can't help but think of the sweet friends who've walked through deep loss and still seem to find pockets of joy in their daily lives. Maybe that's you. If so, you should know I pray for you often, even if I don't always say it. I also think often about your loss and how you balance the joy and the pain. It may look effortless on the outside, but navigating how to let joy and pain co-exist is never easy.

Gratitude and praise are our offering and our way to prepare for fullness of joy. Psalm 16:11 speaks the cry of our joy-seeking hearts,

"You make known to me the path of life; in your presence there is fullness of joy; at your right hand are pleasures forevermore."

That joy extends beyond the full life God promises here and now to our life beyond this world—a life forever in the presence of a joy-giving God who pours into us without restraint. Author, artist, and inspiration Joni Eareckson Tada wrote these words about what joy will be like in heaven. Let's soak in her description as we sum up our chapter on being filled with joy:

> "When I think of my vessel, I picture a gallon bucket into which the Lord will pour His joy until it gushes over the brim, bubbling up and effervescing. I'll laugh with delight for others who will have a joy-capacity the size of a big bathtub, or a tank, truck, or a silo. Like me, they will be filled to overflowing, and we all shall be as happy as cats with nine tails! Whether a small vial or a large vase, we shall all be spilling and splashing over with the joy of the Lord; and even those whose capacity is only the size of a thimble won't know jealousy. We shall be fat, sassy, and satiated with joy. Constant brimming over."[4]

Maybe today we're only able to find a thimble-sized portion of gratitude and praise to offer, and that's okay. God will honor every offering, however small. And in his economy, our most meager gesture will be met with God's joy brimming over.

OUR HEART-FULL PRAYER

Naomi's joyful moment, cradling her new grandbaby in her arms, revealed how God fills his daughters with unspeakable joy. *Joy* represents our ninth measure of blessing God will use to refill our empty spaces. Let's ready our hearts to receive by taking time to praise, pray, and give thanks.

Dear God,

There are days when joy feels like an impossible dream. When the void of loss overpowers any hope for joy restored to my life. Other times, I may have found a brief joyful moment. But without warning, the void returns, reminding me of what's lost. Help me understand your promise to restore to me the joy of my salvation. In you there is fullness of joy, even in times of pain and sorrow. I offer you my gratitude and praise today, Lord. You are a good and faithful God. You bless me beyond measure. As I prepare to receive from your bounty, I can sing of your joy and how it fills my heart. Thank you for understanding my hurt, seeing my tears, and filling me with unspeakable joy. In Jesus' name, Amen.

REFILLED

CHAPTER 11

Jesus Fills Me, This I Know

"And the church is his body; it is made full and complete by Christ, who fills all things everywhere with himself"

EPHESIANS 1:23 NLT

We wrapped up our last chapter in a posture of offering. We stood with Naomi and received an outpouring of grain to fill our cupped hands. Then we turned those hands toward heaven and offered our gratitude and praise for God's continued care and provision. I pray we can remain in this position as we gather to discover our tenth and final measure of blessing God wants to pour into our lives. Gratitude and praise are not the only things we have to offer. Today we join hands, preparing to say goodbye to Naomi and wish her well. Next we look forward to what's coming, and we let our emptiness be our offering. I'd dare to say this final filling will be the most memorable of them all.

"And the women of the neighborhood gave him a name, saying, 'A son has been born to Naomi.' They named him Obed. He was the father of Jesse, the father of David" (Ruth 4:17).

Did Naomi ever think about days past, when she woke up to nothingness and longed for better days? Her current circumstances showed a much more hopeful scene. Instead of opening the front door to a barren land stretched out before her, she could hold Ruth and Boaz's bundle of joy in one arm and bask in the glory of what God had done. The harvest had come.

The Book of Ruth draws to a close with total focus on Naomi, just as it began. I'm so glad the author structured it that way, because the book's conclusion is quite a contrast from the beginning. This no-nonsense woman we've come to know couldn't be more different than she was back then. The writer introduced us to Naomi in chapter one with a relatable description of her emptiness. We identified with her longing for what was and the bitterness in her emptied heart. We empathized with her pain because we've had plenty of our own voids, you and me. We also stayed beside her as she kept taking steps forward, knowing that even small progress is progress, nonetheless.

Now, we near the end of our time together by celebrating her fullness. I love how the account of events include, "A son has been born to Naomi," reminding us that even though it was Ruth who gave birth, Obed's existence brought abundant blessings to Naomi, as well. Blessings have a way of spilling over into more than we ever imagined.

The name Obed means "serving" or "worshiper."[1] Either of these definitions fit like a newborn baby cradled in his doting grandmother's arms. As we saw in the previous passage, the townswomen worshiped God in gratitude and praise for this great gift. Little did anyone suspect, this baby blessing would also serve a crucial role in the lineage leading to God's divine plan for our ultimate good.

"Now these are the generations of Perez: Perez fathered Hezron, Hezron fathered Ram, Ram fathered Amminadab, Amminadab fathered Nahshon, Nahshon fathered Salmon, Salmon fathered Boaz, Boaz fathered Obed, Obed fathered Jesse, and Jesse fathered David" (Ruth 4:18–22).

On the surface, the final few verses may feel lackluster compared to the adventure we've experienced with Naomi, Ruth, and Boaz. Yet underneath it all, buried beneath lesson after lesson on how to let God be our portion when life leaves a void, this most important lesson waited to be uncovered. The simple reciting of Obed's lineage paused at the boy David, who would one day slay giants and become king. For the rest of the story, we only need to flip ahead in our Bibles to Luke 3 or Matthew 1. In either of those places in Scripture, we will find the lineage trail from David to our Savior Jesus. Feel free to take a moment to grab your Bible and turn there now, but if you'd like the summed up version, here you go.

"So all the generations from Abraham to David were fourteen generations, and from David to the deportation to Babylon fourteen generations, and from the deportation to Babylon to the Christ fourteen generations" (Matthew 1:17).

ALL TRAILS END HERE

My husband and I treated ourselves to a spectacular anniversary trip to commemorate our thirty years of marriage. We ventured back to where we spent our honeymoon and planned to check out local hiking spots. Our son and soon to be daughter-in-love introduced us to an app on our phones that would show us trails near our area. We'd be able to check out their distances, difficulty levels, and more. At any time we could see a map with an overview of our current location, where we had been, and how to get to the end of the trail. I found it interesting how there were always different paths to choose from that all ended in the same place. Most times, the trails formed a big loop, taking us back to our starting point.

I imagine what Naomi would've thought if she could have looked at a map of her journey from start to finish to see the series of connecting trails up the steepest mountains and through the deepest valleys. We all have a series of connecting trails, some we took intentionally and others with an accidental wrong turn. But at whatever point in the path, we can look back and see our loving God holding the overview in hand and keeping an eye on us. We never left his line of sight and never ventured beyond his reach. Naomi's hike took her back to her physical home, and that may be true for some of us. Other trails may point us in directions far from where we began. Yet her story reminds us, her return to Bethlehem represented more than physical space. It signified our lifelong journey toward our home with God. No matter how far away we travel, he has already carved out trails that lead back to him.

When we read the end of Naomi's story about the birth of her grandson Obed, our limited hiking expertise might lead us to believe this is the end of the trail. But I'll let you in on something I've learned along the way. Every chapter, verse, and line in Scripture points to Jesus. That's what I think of when I see a story like Naomi's, ending with a list of names. The lineage mentioned in the last few verses hints not at the end, but at a new beginning. So we can look at the conclusion of her story as a course set for even greater things to come. Things like Jesus' birth, his ministry on Earth, his resurrection, and what the empty tomb means for our emptiness today.

REDEEMED

"But now thus says the Lord, he who created you, O Jacob, he who formed you, O Israel: 'Fear not, for I have redeemed you; I have called you by name, you are mine'" (Isaiah 43:1).

Distant memories seem to fade with age, but one memory from childhood remains as clear and crisp as if I'm seeing it right now. Only three or four years old, I'm standing in the church nursery, staring up at an intricate mural on the wall. The artwork, created by my mom, portrayed a boy and girl playing, animals of every shape and size, and a huge tree. That mural represented an important time in my life, when Sunday school teachers saturated me with stories from the Bible and the love of Jesus. I recall getting a red Bible with my name etched on the cover. A special gift, all mine. I also recall John 3:16 as my first memorized verse.

"For God so loved the world, that he gave his only Son, that whoever believes in him should not perish but have eternal life" (John 3:16).

Still, even with the blessing of being introduced to the Bible early in life, it would be many years before I came to know my Savior Jesus in a personal relationship and understand his redeeming work in me. I guess I needed to realize how much I needed a redeemer before I would let go of self-sufficiency and run into his outstretched arms. Full disclosure, he'd been waiting quite a while for me to make that choice, but his arms never fell limp to his sides. He never tired of waiting. It took wandering down some wrong and often dangerous paths before understanding Jesus' way meant freedom from guilt, condemnation, and shame. But a redeemer doesn't ask questions about where you've been and what took you so long. He simply welcomes and celebrates your return.

God knew we would need a redeemer, so he sent his Son to Earth to take our sin and carry it with him to the cross where he would be crucified. As if the cross wasn't heavy enough, in his weakened, tortured state, he added the weight of the sin of each and every person.

All God asks of us is that we would willingly give it to Jesus. Seek his forgiveness. Invite him to live within our hearts. Doesn't seem like a fair trade, does it? That right there demonstrates the role of Redeemer and why no one else would be able to do it. No one else with the compassion, humility, sacrifice, and sinless existence. Only Jesus.

"He has delivered us from the domain of darkness and transferred us to the kingdom of his beloved Son, in whom we have redemption, the forgiveness of sins" (Colossians 1:13–14).

Many similarities exist between Jesus' role as our Redeemer and how Boaz redeemed Ruth and Naomi. Both stories show we are always within reach of a God who loves and cares for us; that God has a plan, even when we can't see beyond the emptiness. The Scriptures clearly demonstrate that our past does not define who we are or limit what God can do through us. But I use caution in drawing too many comparisons, because this book may focus on the life of Naomi and what we can learn from her, but I always, always want the message to point to Jesus. His redemption work is not finished yet, but we have his promise in the empty tomb he left behind. Let's explore this crucial emptiness right now, just as the women did when they first visited the grave of their Lord.

UNFILL MY HEART

"But the angel said to the women, 'Do not be afraid, for I know that you seek Jesus who was crucified. He is not here, for he has risen, as he said. Come, see the place where he lay" (Matthew 28:5–6).

Bible scholars identify the two Marys mentioned in the book of Matthew as Mary Magdalene and Mary, the mother of James and Joseph.[2] Their identities open up vast insight into their relationship with the man called Jesus. These women had been through indescribable things. They'd experienced voids no one could see, hidden away from the ridicule or condemnation the

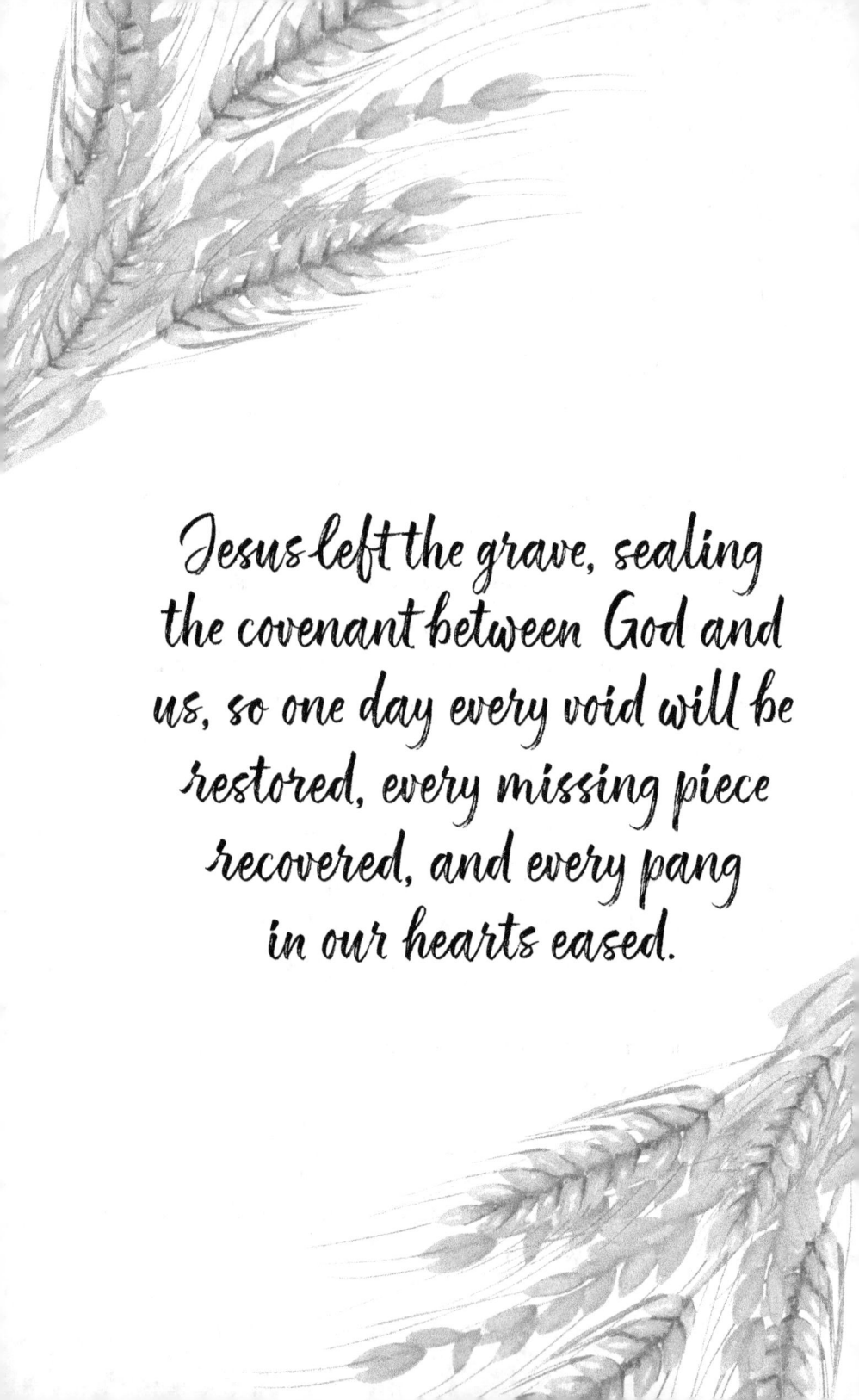

Jesus left the grave, sealing the covenant between God and us, so one day every void will be restored, every missing piece recovered, and every pang in our hearts eased.

CHAPTER 11 — JESUS FILLS ME, THIS I KNOW

world would give. Voids that only Jesus knew of. Maybe that's why they had such a close connection with him. The bond between redeemer and redeemed is a strong one.

Like Naomi, these women once lived with full hearts. Jesus saved them and set them free, yet they walked to the tomb empty and hopeless because of their precious Savior's death. I would have loved to see the shock in their eyes at the first sight of the angel! Even more bewildering than his fiery presence, the words they heard turned everything around. "He is not here…"

I can't say how I would've reacted in their place, but I do know I would've needed the directions repeated a time or two, at least. I would have wanted to linger in the place where Jesus' body lay and soak in my surroundings. My mind would've been transfixed on the truth Jesus tried to tell me that had now come to fruition. But these gutsy ladies did as the angel directed. Their former somber steps now replaced with bountiful joy.

"So the women hurried away from the tomb, afraid yet filled with joy, and ran to tell his disciples" (Matthew 28:8 NIV).

The tomb was empty, yet the women were filled with joy. Let's allow the hope of that statement to change the way we view our own emptiness. The grave opens our lives to renewed possibilities. We have hope for the future because of the empty tomb. Our *measure to remember* is this.

Jesus left the grave, sealing the covenant between God and us, so one day every void will be restored, every missing piece recovered, and every pang in our hearts eased.

FILLED WITH JESUS HIMSELF

"Let the message about Christ, in all its richness, fill your lives" (Colossians 3:16a NLT).

We've come far on our path to finding fulfillment in God and understanding his satisfying portion when life leaves a void on the surface of our hearts. We've also lived long enough to know a life of faith won't always be lush and green. It has and will continue to be dotted with heartache, but thankfully we have the promise of the empty tomb left behind when Jesus rose from the grave. Until the time he returns, we have him in full measure through the Holy Spirit because Jesus fills everything everywhere with himself.

"And the church is his body; it is made full and complete by Christ, who fills all things everywhere with himself" (Ephesians 1:23 NLT).

Paul's words to the Ephesians give us claim to this final promise discovered in our time spent together, following Naomi from emptiness to fullness in God. Jesus fills us with himself, and before he could fill all things, Jesus first emptied himself. "Have this mind among yourselves, which is yours in Christ Jesus, who, though he was in the form of God, did not count equality with God a thing to be grasped, but emptied himself, by taking the form of a servant, being born in the likeness of men. And being found in human form, he humbled himself by becoming obedient to the point of death, even death on a cross" (Philippians 2:5–8). From Jesus' sacrificial example, we can better comprehend the purpose of our empty seasons. We can also better understand where to find the fulfillment our hearts long for.

CHAPTER 11 — JESUS FILLS ME, THIS I KNOW

My fulfillment does not depend upon my circumstances.

My fulfillment does not depend on other people's actions (or inaction).

My fulfillment does not depend on picture-perfect days and a pain-free life.

My fulfillment depends on the promise I find in the empty tomb and the redemptive work of God through Jesus. As we envision Naomi rocking baby Obed to sleep, glancing up at her stocked shelves with a grin, let's hold on to this truth and thank our Lord Jesus for filling us today.

OUR HEART-FULL PRAYER

The tenth measure God will use to fill the void in our hearts is Jesus himself. Before we take our cares to the Lord in this last heart-full prayer, let's take a moment to give thanks for Naomi's life and all we've discovered in our time with her. May her story continue to touch lives and encourage generations to come.

Dear Jesus,

Thank you for emptying yourself and sacrificing everything for me. You didn't deserve to carry the weight of my sins, but you willingly took it with you to the grave. I know you will come again one day. I have that promise because of the empty tomb! Thank you for "filling all things everywhere with yourself." One day I will see you face to face. Until then, I will live in the promise of your presence. Every good and perfect thing was created for you and through you, and we get to enjoy the beauty of your goodness here on Earth. Help me re-

member you are here with me now, ready to wrap me in your tender arms and fill me up. You are my Savior, my Redeemer, and my friend. Amen.

CHAPTER 12

A Life Refilled

*"The LORD is my portion," says my soul,
"therefore I will hope in him"*

LAMENTATIONS 3:24

"For the search for wholeness compels every person, every hour of their lives, whether they know it or not. We ache to be made whole again. And only one Person who ever walked this earth can do this for the heart and soul he created himself" (John Eldredge, *Moving Mountains*).[1]

Much has been said in faith circles about the idea of emptiness, and I feel like I've heard it all. Everything from "God will empty us out" to "we should empty ourselves daily," and honestly, it's a bit exhausting. I know I can say that to you without judgement because we've come to know each other well, so you know I'm not all about discussing theological differences to death. I hope with all hope you sensed my care and concern for you as I poured out my heart on each and every page. I also hope the messages shared gave you solace for times when your heart is full and even when it's not. This book has not been about embracing emptiness so we can get something from God or filling ourselves with meaningless things instead. No, my fellow camper, it has been about so much more than I could have planned or expected when I began to research, study, and write.

One of my favorite activities along our journey had to be praying together through the *Heart-Full Prayers* at the end of the chapters. For this final chapter I felt it fitting to give you a space to write your own heart-full prayer. You can find it in Appendix A in the back of the book. Don't let yourself get bogged down with the right words, just allow the empty space to beckon you to give it all to God.

To put the last piece in place and complete this intricate picture God has been creating for us, let's take a quick look at where it all began in chapter one, before we met our new friend Naomi in the Book of Ruth.

I took you back to a memory from my own life, watching a movie where a scene played out of young campers forced by the camp Warden to dig hole after hole in an unforgiving, dried-up lake bed. I admitted my own holes—the ones invisible to others but taking up space on the surface of my heart. We searched together for our voids and thought about the recurring pain they brought back time and again. We discovered what it means to let God be our portion, in want and in plenty, through verses

CHAPTER 12 — A LIFE REFILLED

in God's Word, like Psalm 16:5, "The Lord is my chosen portion and my cup; you hold my lot." We dealt with our bitterness, then we let ourselves lean into the voids a bit more, even though it was scary at times. The idea of living with God as our portion is echoed in Lamentations 3:24, "'The LORD is my portion,' says my soul, 'therefore I will hope in him.'" That is my soul's cry right now. *God, you are my portion. Today, tomorrow, forever.* For the purposes of this book, the Contemporary English Version puts it well, "Deep in my heart I say, 'The Lord is all I need; I can depend on him!'"

In the deepest recesses of our cavernous hearts, God resides with the purpose of filling us with all the goodness of his existence. He is all we need, so let's commit to total dependence on him to be our never-ending source. Here's a recap of the ten measures of blessing God will use to fill our empty spaces. God promises to fill us with:

Love

Peace

Good things

Strength

Grace

The Spirit of God

Abundance

Light

Joy

Jesus

Seeing all these amazing gifts listed above refreshes my spirit in ways I can hardly contain. I pray you feel it, too! We are seen and cared for by an awesome God, perfect in character and generous by nature. I can think of nothing else more satisfying than that.

DISCOVERING FULLNESS IN GOD

Ever notice how you can tell where a hole once was? Years ago our nine-year-old and his friend from the neighborhood took advantage of the new construction and sandy soil in the backyard by digging the deepest hole they could. The hole grew so big, pretty soon I could only see their heads and shoulders popping up as I called to them from the back door.

Their faces sank the day I made them fill it up, but they conceded. For months after that fateful day, the fresh mound of dirt reminded us about the once-dug hole. We had a constant memorial of where it had been. Soon, various wildflowers dotted the top of the mound, trying to hide its existence but instead creating something new. The boys learned a valuable truth about empty space—one Naomi learned, and over time, a lesson God will seal in our spirits. A dug hole can never be undug; it can only be refilled, but that doesn't make it any less beautiful.

The word *fullness* can be defined as, "the state of being filled to capacity" or "the state of being complete or whole."[2] These two definitions speak to my searching soul that longs for understanding, especially as it relates to the idea of fullness in God. They create a picture of a hole filled as full as it can possibly get. But to get the complete picture of God's role in our potential for fullness, we need to look at the word from a biblical view. *Fullness* is used in Scripture in various ways. Let's pack up our tents with this one final verse as we prepare to bring the message home.

God wants us
to be whole.

". . . so that Christ may dwell in your hearts through faith—that you, being rooted and grounded in love, may have strength to comprehend with all the saints what is the breadth and length and height and depth, and to know the love of Christ that surpasses knowledge, *that you may be filled with all the fullness of God*" (Ephesians 3:17–19, Emphasis mine).

The *International Standard Bible Encyclopedia* encourages us, "that ye may be wholly filled with God and with His presence and power and grace." The entry goes on to say this about fullness in the Bible, "This is the fullness of the nature of God—life, light, love; and this has its permanent, its settled abode in Christ. All that is His own by right is His by His Father's good pleasure also."[3]

Throughout the writing of this book, I've often paused to ponder the one most important thing I'd like you to remember from Naomi's life. The one truth I desire for us to walk away with and never forget is simple. If you leave with nothing else, I want you to know this.

God wants us to be whole.

He wants us to be well, healed, content, satisfied, grateful, and complete. He also gets us. He understands we will have times when we don't feel whole, but if we can grasp this truth with both hands and learn to return to him empty, God will not only fill us. He will fill us to overflowing.

MOVING FORWARD

I always hated the last day of camp. As a young girl, I was prone to homesickness. I couldn't wait for my mom to show up, offer

CHAPTER 12 — A LIFE REFILLED

a big hug, and take me home to a good meal and a good night's sleep in my own bed. But that meant saying goodbye to new friends and realizing we wouldn't see each other for another year. (This, of course, was before computers and cell phones.) I'm hoping this is not goodbye for us, either. In fact, in an effort to keep the connection going, I've listed a few ways you can stay in touch with me in the back of the book. You'll find them in the Appendix section. And speaking of our hopes and prayers, I have a few for us moving forward. We've learned all the lessons, bared our hurts, and gained renewed dependence on our heavenly Father. Closing the last page of the last chapter of a book is no fun, but if there's one thing our time together has uncovered, it's that real growth happens when we apply what we've learned to our everyday lives. Here are my hopes and prayers for us in the coming days, weeks, and months:

- That we won't let our problems seem so big that they take up more space in our heart than God does.

- That we will resist the temptation to fill the void in our heart with our own strength, and that we will trust God with the process.

- That we will see incredible potential, not in spite of the void, but because of what God will do with it.

- That we will know each void in our heart is not something to be avoided, despised, or feared, but as God refills us, it will become part of our beautiful ongoing story.

So you might be saying, "I'm not ready for the next empty space, the next void." You might even be apprehensive about taking this message to heart for fear of what's ahead for you. If that describes you, then I want you to do one more thing for me. I want you to think of the image of an overfilled hole covered in flowers of bright hues of yellow and blue, and I want you to think of God's desire for your fullness. Because you're right. A hole in our hearts will not return to its former condition, as much as we wish it would. Even when it's filled, you can tell it's still there. But what God wants to bring to the void will create beauty where we never thought possible. Courage in the chasm of fear. Love in the wasteland of bitterness. Light in the dark hole of loneliness. Joy in the depth of grief. A harvest in the midst of nothingness. Today as we change how we look at the void in our hearts and let God be our refilling Source, we will discover renewed possibility for when life leaves us empty. We will be able to say with gratitude and resolve, "God is the portion for my empty spaces, and because of him, I can live refilled."

REFILLED

Appendix A
Reflection Pages

To download a printable version of
these Reflection Pages, visit *refilledbook.com*

CHAPTER 1: EMPTY SPACES

In this chapter, I discovered that God is _____

Find the measure to remember for this chapter and write it below.

_____

_____

Write out the verse from this chapter that speaks to you most in this season of your life. _____

_____

_____

_____

What circumstance in your life—past or present—has left behind a void, causing a feeling of emptiness?

_____

_____

_____

_____

If I asked you what it means to live with God as your portion, what would you say?

_____

_____

_____

_____

One thing I will remember about Naomi is _____

_____

CHAPTER 2: THE LONELY HEART CLUB

In this chapter, I discovered that God fills me with _____

Find the measure to remember for this chapter and write it below.

_____

_____

Write out the verse from this chapter that speaks to you most in this season of your life. _____

_____

_____

_____

Is there a time in your life when you experienced feelings of separation or loneliness? Reread this verse from the chapter: "But you, O Lord, are a God merciful and gracious, slow to anger and abounding in steadfast love and faithfulness" (Psalm 86:15). How do these words speak to times of isolation in our lives?

_____

_____

_____

_____

In this chapter, we learn that God will pour his never-ending love into our hearts. Think of that truth in light of your lonely times. What new revelation do you have about God's love from this part of Naomi and Elimelech's story?

_____

_____

_____

_____

One thing I will remember about Naomi is _____

_____

CHAPTER 3: A LITTLE LESS FULL

In this chapter, I discovered that God fills me with _____

Find the measure to remember for this chapter and write it below.

Write out the verse from this chapter that speaks to you most in this season of your life.

Are you in a *heart-full* season or *a little less full* season? Use the space below to journal about your current season and how you sense God's presence in the midst of it.

Read John 14:27 in different versions of the Bible. How does Jesus' peace differ from the peace the world offers?

One thing I will remember about Naomi is _____

CHAPTER 4: AN OMER OF GOOD THINGS

In this chapter, I discovered that God fills me with _____

Find the measure to remember for this chapter and write it below.

_____

_____

Write out the verse from this chapter that speaks to you most in this season of your life. _____

_____

_____

_____

How does the widow of Zarephath's story impact your idea about God's supply?

_____

_____

_____

_____

Reread the Hebrew measurement descriptions in this chapter. Sometimes in our lives, God provides an omer. Other times, he pours out an abundance. What might God want us to learn about his character as our Great Provider? In what specific area of your life do you need God's provision today?

_____

_____

_____

_____

One thing I will remember about Naomi is _____

_____

CHAPTER 5: GIVE ME STRENGTH!

In this chapter, I discovered that God fills me with _____

Find the measure to remember for this chapter and write it below.

_____

_____

Write out the verse from this chapter that speaks to you most in this season of your life. _____

_____

_____

_____

God promised Moses rest. Reread this verse: "And he said, 'My presence will go with you, and I will give you rest'" (Exodus 33:14). In what ways does this verse comfort you when you're exhausted? Write a short prayer thanking God for his gift of rest.

_____

_____

_____

_____

We discovered in this chapter how pain or illness can chip away at a void in our hearts. What are some ways you can stay spiritually nourished? In what areas of your life do you need a refilling of God's strength?

_____

_____

_____

_____

One thing I will remember about Naomi is _____

_____

CHAPTER 6: BITTER WOMAN

In this chapter, I discovered that God fills me with _____

Find the measure to remember for this chapter and write it below.

_____

_____

Write out the verse from this chapter that speaks to you most in this season of your life. _____

_____

_____

_____

Has an incident or circumstance ever led to a buildup of bitterness that made you feel like a different person?

_____

_____

_____

_____

Are you struggling to get past the hurt someone else caused? Have you felt abandoned by God or wondered if he cares about your situation?

_____

_____

_____

_____

One thing I will remember about Naomi is _____

_____

CHAPTER 7: SO, HELP ME, GOD

In this chapter, I discovered that God fills me with _____

Find the measure to remember for this chapter and write it below.

_____

_____

Write out the verse from this chapter that speaks to you most in this season of your life. _____

_____

_____

_____

The same Spirit that gave courage to Joshua, faith to Gideon, strength to Samson, and wisdom to Bezalel, is here and ready to step into our emptiness. In this chapter, we saw how the Holy Spirit empowered people in the Old Testament for a specific purpose. Think about the Holy Spirit's role in your life today. List ways in which the Holy Spirit has empowered you.

_____

_____

_____

_____

Write a short prayer asking the Holy Spirit to fill you according to God's perfect will.

_____

_____

_____

_____

One thing I will remember about Naomi is _____

_____

CHAPTER 8: EVEN MORE

In this chapter, I discovered that God fills me with _____

Find the measure to remember for this chapter and write it below.

_____

_____

Write out the verse from this chapter that speaks to you most in this season of your life. _____

_____

_____

_____

In what ways did God show himself to be a Master Restorer in Naomi's life and the lives of her people?

_____

_____

_____

_____

Would you consider yourself in an abundant season or a scarce season right now? What do you need to release to God, the Master Restorer?

_____

_____

_____

_____

One thing I will remember about Naomi is _____

_____

CHAPTER 9: IN A NEW LIGHT

In this chapter, I discovered that God fills me with _____

Find the measure to remember for this chapter and write it below.

_____

_____

Write out the verse from this chapter that speaks to you most in this season of your life. _____

_____

_____

_____

What seasons of the past do you miss most? In what ways has God reminded you of his goodness in your current season?

_____

_____

_____

_____

How has God illuminated your heart through the lessons in this chapter? How can we relate Naomi's earthly inheritance to our spiritual inheritance as God's children?

_____

_____

_____

_____

One thing I will remember about Naomi is _____

_____

CHAPTER 10: DOWN IN MY HEART, WHERE?

In this chapter, I discovered that God fills me with _____

Find the measure to remember for this chapter and write it below.

_____

_____

Write out the verse from this chapter that speaks to you most in this season of your life. _____

_____

_____

_____

Have you ever been in the midst of a joyful season when the pain of the void returned? Jot down how it made you feel. What truth from God's Word will help you when this happens?

_____

_____

_____

_____

What can we do to prepare our hearts for joy?

_____

_____

_____

_____

One thing I will remember about Naomi is _____

_____

CHAPTER 11: JESUS FILLS ME, THIS I KNOW

In this chapter, I discovered that God fills me with _____

Find the measure to remember for this chapter and write it below.

_____

_____

Write out the verse from this chapter that speaks to you most in this season of your life. _____

_____

_____

_____

How can we identify with the women at Jesus' tomb? What would you like to say to Jesus right now? Write your thoughts here.

_____

_____

_____

_____

The apostle Paul said Jesus fills all things everywhere with himself. What does that promise mean for you and your life today?

_____

_____

_____

_____

One thing I will remember about Naomi is _____

_____

CHAPTER 12: A LIFE REFILLED

Write out your personal prayer for receiving God's sustaining portion.

My Personal Heart-Full Prayer

Appendix B
Book Club Reading Plan

Are you a member of a book club or women's group that would enjoy reading *Refilled* together? Follow this simple plan to read through the book in one month as a group.

- **Week One**   Introduction & Chapters 1–3
- **Week Two**   Chapters 4–6
- **Week Three** Chapters 7–9
- **Week Four**   Chapters 10–12

Create a special time for your group by wrapping up the month with a *Refilled* get-together and discussion! Visit the book's web page at *refilledbook.com* for ideas, along with other free book club and small group resources.

NOTES

CHAPTER 1 — EMPTY SPACES

1. Davis, Andrew. 2003. *Holes*. United States: Buena Vista Pictures, 2 hrs. DVD.
2. Davis, Andrew. 2003. *Holes*. United States: Buena Vista Pictures, 2 hrs. DVD.
3. Definition of the word "filled." *Life Application Study Bible, NLT, Dictionary/Concordance,* Tyndale House Publishers, Carol Stream, IL, 2015.
4. Numbers 13:27.
5. Hebrew word for "lot." Note on Psalm 16:5, *NIV Exhaustive Concordance Dictionary*. Copyright © 2015 by Zondervan.

CHAPTER 2 — THE LONELY HEART CLUB

1. Note on "famine" in *Essential Bible Dictionary*, Zondervan, 2011, accessed https://biblegateway.com, May 5, 2024.
2. Numbers 14:33–34.
3. Note on Ruth 1:1, *NIV Study Bible*, Zondervan, Grand Rapids, MI, 1995.
4. Exodus 14.
5. Joshua 6.
6. Note on Ruth 1:2, *Matthew Henry Commentary*, https://biblegateway.com, accessed May 5, 2024.
7. Smith, William, Dr. "Entry for 'Ephrathite.'" *Smith's Bible Dictionary*, 1901.
8. *Easton's Bible Dictionary*, "Entries for Bethlehem and Ephrathah." https://Biblehub.com, accessed May 5, 2024.
9. Map, *The ESV Global Study Bible*, ESV Bible Copyright 2012 by Crossway. All rights reserved. Accessed May 5, 2024, https://biblegateway.com.
10. Numbers 25:9.
11. Genesis 19:37.
12. Ninan, Mabel, *Far from Home*, pg. 9, Iron Stream Media, Birmingham, AL, 2022.

CHAPTER 3 — A LITTLE LESS FULL

1. Brown, Kristine, *Cinched: Living with Unwavering Trust in an Unfailing God*, Aberdeen Books LLC, Tyler, TX, 2021.
2. McDonald, Abby, "How Do We Survive Grief for Someone Who Is Still Living" https://abbymcdonald.org/2018/04/when-we-grieve-the-living/, April 12, 2018.

CHAPTER 4 — AN OMER OF GOOD THINGS

1. Note on Ruth 1:3, *NIV Cultural Backgrounds Study Bible*, https://biblegateway.com, accessed May 1, 2024.
2. *NIV Exhaustive Concordance Dictionary*. Copyright © 2015 by Zondervan, https://biblegateway.com, accessed May 1, 2024.

CHAPTER 5 — GIVE ME STRENGTH!

1. Note on Ruth 1:3, *NIV Cultural Backgrounds Study Bible*, Copyright © 2016 by Zondervan. Accessed May 1, 2024.
2. Note on *Strong's H4496,* Blue Letter Bible, https://www.blueletterbible.org/lexicon/h4496/esv/wlc/0-1/, accessed May 12, 2024.
3. Note on Ruth 1:8, *NIV Cultural Backgrounds Study Bible*, https://biblegateway.com, accessed May 17, 2024.
4. Brown, Kristine, *Cinched*, pg. 90, Aberdeen Books, Tyler, TX, 2021.
5. Marcora SM, Staiano W, Manning V. "Mental fatigue impairs physical performance in humans." J Appl Physiol (1985). 2009 Mar;106(3):857–64. doi: 10.1152/japplphysiol.91324.2008. Epub 2009 Jan 8. PMID: 19131473.
6. Sheer Watters, Judy, YouTube channel: You Have a Story to Tell Episode: "Memoir Writing Prompt #49: A Difficult Time in Your Life" https://www.youtube.com/watch?v=O4_4xH-u8lk&t=174s, July 11, 2023.

CHAPTER 6 — BITTER WOMAN

1. Norton, Mark R., Swanson, James A., *NIV Exhaustive Concordance Dictionary*. Copyright 2015 by Zondervan. Accessed on https://biblegateway.com, May 23, 2024.
2. "Introduction to Zechariah Timeline" *NIV Study Bible 10th Anniversary Edition*, Zondervan, 1985.
3. Brown, Kristine, "God Knew We Would Need Grace." April 26, 2022, www.sweettothesoul.com/blog/2022/04/26/god-knew-we-would-need-grace
4. *Zondervan Illustrated Bible Backgrounds Commentary of the Old Testament*, Copyright 2002. Accessed https://biblegateway.com, October 25, 2022.

CHAPTER 7 — SO, HELP ME, GOD

1. Stinson, Michelle, "Food, Festivals, and the Book of Ruth" September 1, 2022. tyndalehouse.com/explore/articles/food-festivals-and-the-book-of-ruth/
2. Stinson, Michelle, "Food, Festivals, and the Book of Ruth" September 1, 2022. tyndalehouse.com/explore/articles/food-festivals-and-the-book-of-ruth/
3. *Easton's Bible Dictionary*, note on "barley." Accessed May 23, 2024, https://biblegateway.com.

4   Appelo, Lisa. *Life Can Be Good Again*, Bethany House Publishers, Minneapolis, MN, 2022, p. 159.
5   Guzik, David. "Were Old Testament Believers Filled with the Holy Spirit?" no pub date, accessed June 4, 2024. https://enduringword.com/were-old-testament-believers-filled-with-the-holy-spirit/.
6   Judges 14:6.
7   1 Samuel 10:9–10.
8   Numbers 27:18.
9   Guzik, David. "Were Old Testament Believers Filled with the Holy Spirit?" no pub date, accessed June 4, 2024. https://enduringword.com/were-old-testament-believers-filled-with-the-holy-spirit/
10 Note on Deuteronomy 14:29, *Strong's Concordance*, Accessed June 20, 2024. Blue Letter Bible https://www.blueletterbible.org/lexicon/h7646/esv/wlc/0-1/.

CHAPTER 8 — EVEN MORE

1   Note on Ruth 3:2, *NIV Study Bible 10th Anniversary Edition*, Marvin R. Wilson, John H. Stek, eds., The Zondervan Corporation, 1995.
2   Stinson, Michelle, "Food Festivals and the Book of Ruth." September 1, 2022, https://Tyndalehouse.com, accessed June 30, 2024.
3   Note on Joel 2:18, *NLT Life Application Study Bible*, Tyndale House Publishers, Carol Stream, IL, 2015.
4   Note on Psalm 65:6–13, *NLT Life Application Study Bible,* Tyndale House Publishers, 2015., Carol Stream, IL. 2015.
5   Note on "barley," *Easton's Bible Dictionary*. Accessed May 27, 2024, https://biblehub.com/topical/b/barley.htm.
6   Note on Ruth 3:, *NIV Study Bible 10th Anniversary Edition*, Marvin R. Wilson, John H. Stek, eds., The Zondervan Corporation, 1995.

CHAPTER 9 — IN A NEW LIGHT

no notes for this chapter

CHAPTER 10 — DOWN IN MY HEART, WHERE?

1   Henley, Marissa. "A Bold Prayer" Ruth Bible Study, First 5 app, 2023, https://app.first5.org/book/Ruth%202023/ff_ruth23_23.
2   Note on 126:1, *Expositor's Bible Commentary*, https://biblegateway.com, accessed July 20, 2024.
3   Swift, Doris, *Surrender the Joy Stealers*, pg. 19, Elk Lake Publishing, Inc., Plymouth, MA, 2023.
4   Eareckson Tada, Joni, *Heaven, Your Real Home*, pg. 90, Zondervan Publishing House, Grand Rapids, MI, 1995.

CHAPTER 11 — JESUS FILLS ME, THIS I KNOW

1. Note on Obed, *Strong's Concordance*, Blue Letter Bible, accessed July 25, 2024. https://www.blueletterbible.org/lexicon/h5744/esv/wlc/0-1/
2. Note on Matthew 28. *Zondervan Illustrated Bible Backgrounds Commentary of the New Testament*, Copyright 2002. Accessed https://biblegateway.com, July 29, 2024.

CHAPTER 12 — A LIFE REFILLED

1. Eldredge, John. *Moving Mountains*, pg. 190, Nelson Books, an imprint of Thomas Nelson, Nashville, TN, 2016.
2. "Fullness" definition, *Oxford Languages*, Copyright © 2024 Oxford University Press. Accessed July 20, 2024.
3. Rutherford, John. "Entry for 'FULLNESS,'" *International Standard Bible Encyclopedia*, 1915. Accessed July 20, 2024. www.blueletterbible.org/search/Dictionary/viewTopic.cfm?topic=IT0003597

Acknowledgments

Writing for the Lord brings me great joy. It also brings a sense of deep responsibility to do the work he has called me to do with humility, obedience, and excellence. I know I cannot do it without being aligned with the Holy Spirit. I would never want to share anything that is not from him. So, I give my God praise and honor for leading me through the writing of this book. My greatest prayer now is that it brings hope and inspiration to those who read it.

Writing can feel like a lonely endeavor. Without the support of friends who know what that life is like, this book would not have been written. My Voxer buddies, Bloggers Unite group, and His Girls Gather crew, your connection gives me the encouragement I need to take brave steps forward when I want to quit. I love you all dearly and pray other writers will find the same connection and friendship I have found in you.

Writers can be a little too critical of themselves. We want our writing to be the best it can be because we care about our readers and want to provide quality inspiration for each person who picks up our books. It's a challenge to look at our own writing subjectively, which is why the right editor can make all the difference in a writer's life by polishing, suggesting, and cheering on in times of doubt. Elizabeth, your partnership as my editor has meant more to me than you know. Thank you for helping make this message of my heart the absolute best it can be.

My Refilled Focus Group, I reached out to you, and you answered the call. You gave your time and wisdom in pondering my questions and providing insight to ensure the integrity of this book for the women who would one day turn its pages. You ensured the message would resonate with readers by holding me accountable to the ideas, stories, and verses I included. I appreciate your contribution more than I can express.

And of course, my family, my heart is full thinking about you as I write these words. Thank you for allowing me to share our stories. That smile you see on my face? It's there because of you. Your support and love mean the world to me.

Connect
WITH KRISTINE

Subscribe to her website
morethanyourself.com

Join her free email studies
morethanyourself.com/email-challenges-kristine-brown

Interact at her YouTube channel
youtube.com/@kristinebrown

Other Books
BY KRISTINE BROWN

Available at Amazon, Barnes & Noble, or your favorite online retailer.

Over It uncovers the solution to the comparison battle all women face.

companion workbook

Cinched guides women in learning to trust God like we mean it.

Over It: Devotional for Teen Girls offers help and hope in the comparison battle teen girls face.